D0836872

—THE—
SECRET
LIFE OF
FOOD

— THE —
SECRET
LIFE OF
FOOD

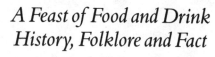

A Feast of Food and Drink
History, Folklore and Fact

Martin Elkort

JEREMY P. TARCHER
Los Angeles

Library of Congress Cataloging in Publication Data

Elkort, Martin Edward.
    The secret life of food : a feast of food and drink history,
  folklore, and fact / Martin Edward Elkort.
        p.   cm.
    Includes bibliographical references and index.
    ISBN 0-87477-662-7
    1. Food—History.   2. Beverages—History.   I. Title
  TX355.E45   1991
  641.3 ' 09—dc20   91-22176
                                                    CIP

Jeremy P. Tarcher, Inc.
5858 Wilshire Blvd., Suite 200
Los Angeles, CA 90036

Design by Lee Fukui
Illustrations by Martin Elkort

Manufactured in the United States of America
10   9   8   7   6   5   4   3   2

This book is dedicated to nine people,
all of whom I love in different ways:
Edythe, who let me write
when I should have been doing other things;
My parents, Lou and Esther Elkort, who never doubted;
My children: Stefani, Daniel, and Alicia;
My friend Murray Vidockler, who always knew;
and my grandchildren:
Evan and Perry Twyford,
for whom the adventure of books is just beginning.

Contents

Acknowledgments

Thank you to beer historian Alan Eames, for generously sharing his knowledge; to food scientist Albert Spiel, whose recollections of the soybean protein revolution are set down here for the first time; to Adriana Pacifici, for her knowledge of cooking and Italians; to William Handwerker of Nathan's Famous for rare information about his grandfather, Nathan Handwerker; to Warren Allen, Secretary of the Lewis County (New York) Maple Producer's Association, for his insights into the world of maple syrup.

Thank you to my editor, Daniel Malvin, at Jeremy P. Tarcher, Inc., for his patience and guidance. Thanks to Jennifer Boynton, production editor, for helping to make this a beautiful book to read. Thank you to my daughter, Alicia, for all the time spent poring over the manuscript, and for her valuable contributions.

Thanks to my agent, Daniel Kaufman, whose enthusiasm made problems melt away.

Introduction

Life is like an onion.
You peel it off one layer at a time;
and sometimes you weep.

Carl Sandburg

Eat to live! The overriding command of all living creatures is activated at birth when the embryo leaves the warm embrace of the amniotic sac and emerges into the cold world. Survival is immediately and painfully threatened by the shock of a severed umbilical cord. Nevermore will nourishment be delivered automatically through a built-in tube in the belly.

The pain and shock at the removal of assured security outrages the baby, who screams in protest. Soon it finds the mother's breast and begins suckling, a satisfying but uncertain replacement for the life-support system of the womb.

The search for food begins. For the rest of our lives the beast in our stomach signals hunger by growling and clawing. It forces the brain to abandon all other thoughts until it is satiated, and makes it throb with the strain of satisfying its demands. Some still the commotion by surrounding the cage with impenetrable walls of sound-deadening fat, endlessly tossing little treats into the gaping maw to placate the monster in the dungeon. Others try to starve it into submission with an iron regimen of diet and aerobics. Still, assured of a steady supply of food, the monster eventually subsides and allows a more playful creature to emerge—the appetite: part intellect, part fashion-follower, part sensualist, part esthete. Once survival is no longer the problem, food can become an art form, a social statement, and an intellectual fulfillment.

Tracing the History of Food

Food is a given; we must eat to live. Much of our time on earth is devoted to hunting and gathering (now called shopping), farming, storing, cooking, and eating food. We push it into our mouths, break it up with our teeth, chew it, swallow it, and let the digestive system take over, sending some to our life engines, converting others into chemicals that do various tasks inside our bodies, storing water and fats against the future, and sending the rest back to the world as excrement. Yet, as vitally important as food is, it has been taken for granted throughout much of history.

The cultural history of food may often be obscure. Musicians were taught by music teachers, who were taught by music teachers who, in turn, were taught by music teachers, all the way back to Bach, Mozart, and Beethoven. With a little careful study one can trace the whole flowering of Western music almost by moving from teacher to composer. Nothing like this exists in the world of food. Only fairly recently has cooking been formally taught. How many cooks can trace their learning to Escoffier, Soyer, Carême, Brillat-Savarin—except through books? And what of the centuries before?

Musicians are worshiped, photographed as they work, interviewed endlessly, and glorified on television interview shows, while famous chefs are bundled into their aprons and banished to the kitchen. If they do make it on television, it is in the late afternoon when no one is watching. There they entertain viewers with cute anecdotes in charming accents in return for permission to promote their books. Is feeding the stomach less important to the survival of the species than feeding the ear?

Napoleon's observation that an army moves on its stomach trivializes a greater truth: civilization moves on its stomach. Trade routes, agriculture, spices, and salt have spawned war and conquest over the years. The accumulation of knowledge, the building of great cities, advances in manufacturing, business, science, and statesmanship, have all resulted from efforts to provide the communal belly with more, or better, fodder. Moses sent spies into Canaan to see if there was enough food there to sustain his tribe. They came back with stories of a bountiful land of milk and honey and brought back luscious grapes to prove it. Since then, wars have been fought over food, the earth has been explored and settled in search of it, fortunes have been made and lost because of it, and inventors of machines to make the gathering and processing of food easier have been immortalized on postage stamps. "Happiness," said a wise man, "begins with a good meal."

But food has been linked to power in another sense: the secret properties of certain foods and the powers they may bestow. In Sri Lanka there is a living fig tree grown from a cutting said to come from the very tree that the great Buddha sat under when he had his world-transforming vision. If one ate of that fig tree, would the wisdom of Buddha be transmitted? There was an olive tree in Greece (until it was demolished by a truck a few years ago) believed to be the one that Socrates sat under as he argued with his disciples two millennia ago. Did the olives from that tree inspire those who ate them?

Unencumbered by facts, the ancients delighted in such speculation. They ate the organs of animals in the belief that the healthy qualities of animal kidneys, brains, and other parts would be absorbed by the human body, making one smarter, stronger, or cured of illness. The cannibal assumed the power of his enemy by eating him. Why are we made of meat, he might have reasoned, if not to eat each other?

We can laugh at the assumptions of yesterday: walnut meat is shaped like brains so eating it will make you smarter. Some of these assumptions even worked themselves into the language. The brain-shaped walnut was possibly responsible for the slang term *nut,* meaning head. A crazy man was a *nut,* or *went nuts.* In business the *nut* is the monthly or yearly amount of money needed to keep the business afloat, an irreducible minimum. *Nut* is also the name of a machine part that keeps other things from falling apart. The word *nut* comes from the Latin *nutriens,* to nourish.

Yet ancient herbal medicines and folk remedies are increasingly accepted by modern medicine. The science mule that moves only when hit over the head by empirical evidence often lags behind public intuition. Today, scientists probe the onion, lemon, and other foods for new cures, and are discovering that many fruits and vegetables contain miraculous substances, ones that often have been used in traditional folk-medicine for centuries.

New developments in archaeology, anthropology, and paleontology allow us to see how cavemen and dinosaurs lived by examining fossilized feces, skeletal teeth, microscopic seeds, and the contents of frozen mastodon stomachs to discover what they ate and what diseases afflicted them. As the secrets of human genes yield to scientific inquiry and new electronic tools become available, the new Rosetta Stones will give us the keys to knowledge once thought lost forever.

Much of food's history, on the other hand, is a great deal more accessible. The birth of the restaurant, for example. As a new middle class coalesced from the ruins of the French Revolution, an unemployed chef named Boulanger opened a kitchen for the public in which he prepared and sold food to take home. His restorative broth, called *restaurant,* was so popular (and he so eager to capitalize on the brisk trade) that he set out a few tables and chairs, wrote on a slate what he was serving and the price, and prepared meals to order, to be consumed on the premises by those able to afford the modest cost. Although various forms of pre-cooked food were available to the public throughout the Middle Ages, historians generally credit the birth of the true restaurant as it exists today to Boulanger. Dining out quickly became fashionable.

Boulanger's *restaurant* was copied by dozens of other unemployed chefs who only months before were preparing *pièce de résistance* for the now-headless ruling class. (Rest assured, however, that the French empire lives on in microcosm in the kitchen of every French restaurant, where the chef is absolute

4

ruler, imperiously running his kingdom, lionized by patrons and staff alike.) Soon, there were restaurants in every large city.

Boulanger got things off to a good start, but cooking at home, particularly in the crowded, working-class neighborhoods of the burgeoning cities, was difficult at best. It was still not possible to store food for easy preparation without using the traditional methods of spicing, pickling, smoking, cold storage (the ice-box), or dehydration, all of which were becoming increasingly impractical. The invention in 1810 by another Frenchman, Nicholas Appert, of the hermetically sealed glass jar, coupled with the innovation of Brian Donkin, an Englishman who gave the world the tin can two years later, made it possible for an unskilled homemaker to fry some meat in a skillet, douse it with bottled sauce, open a few tins of vegetables, and serve a wonderful meal (relatively speaking) to an amazed mate.

The French, who often made their sauces only moments before serving, were appalled at how the English took to their new bottles and tins, pouring all sorts of prepared sauces over canned food to improve the flavor. Despite, however, the French abhorrence of their cooking habits, the English had more important things to do than dither in the kitchen. They had an empire to build, after all. (With the empire now a fading memory, the English are at last turning their attention to the proper preparation of food. They have a long way to go to rectify the damage they did to their cuisine during the halcyon days of empire, but they are manfully—and womanfully—storming the self-made barricades of their international reputation as disastrous cooks.)

It appears the middle class is here to stay, with new recruits joining up all around the world. And with the middle class comes cookbooks. Apicius, a gourmet who clattered around the kitchen in the first century A.D. wrote the Western world's first cookbook for the middle class of the Roman Empire. Since then, thousands of cookbooks have instructed, inspired, and entertained us, not to mention magazines specializing in cooking, dining, and the accessories required to sustain it all. It is a multi-million dollar industry, becoming ever more specialized and complex. In Los Angeles, New York, and other cities, bookstores flourish that sell only books about cooking and the preparation of food. The numbers and girths of underpaid and overfed food critics swell daily. Every newspaper has a dining column in which the food critic bestows his or her rating on the fortunate, or unfortunate, eateries.

Kitchen experimenters can buy cookbooks devoted solely to how to make the best chili and can reinforce their specialized interest with books that deal only with hot peppers, herbs, or other minutiae. Books abound on the effect of food on health, sex, and other matters. There's even a book about how to make cosmetics from ingredients found at the grocery store.

But most of this vast body of literature tells us little about *why* we eat what we do. Why do Chileans and Japanese love sea food? Why must rice (and/or noodles) accompany every meal in Japan, China, and other Asian countries? What makes Teutonic peoples fond of sausages and beer? Why can't Italians stop eating pasta for a while, and switch to something else? What's so wonderful about kippers to an Englishman? Snails to a Frenchman? Yams to an African?

Some restaurants in Guatemala feature what they call "The National Soup" on their menus: black bean soup, the ubiquitous bowl of legumes beloved by *Centro-Americanos*. It is not difficult to visualize the state seal of Guatemala with a steaming bowl of black bean soup rampant against a field of bean plants: the national soup—to some a resource worth defending with honor and life. Loyalty to traditional foods borders on an act of patriotism in some countries. The connection between cuisine and country is natural. The food eaten from childhood through old age, and the way it is prepared, is associated with the most basic events of life: ceremonies and passages, feasts, holidays, family gatherings, national and religious holidays, and happy occasions like picnics and sporting events.

The decorations in many ethnic restaurants are meant partly to assure the patrons that the food served is "authentic," but perhaps a stronger motivation for many is to surround the diner with artifacts and paintings to evoke the ambience of their homeland. Even when traveling through Europe and surrounded by some of the best food establishments in the world, many Americans still find themselves yearning for a hamburger. The craving for indigenous food is a powerful expression of homesickness, love of country, and often, patriotism. When people leave their country of birth they take their cultural heritage with them, including a predilection to certain foods. No matter how complicated a national cuisine becomes, its origin (and thus its predilections) is rooted in something quite simple: use what is close to hand and prepare it with what's available. Add to this equation the strangers who show up with something new to drop into the pot.

Chile averages one hundred miles wide and twenty-five hundred miles long, with a seacoast on one long side and a mountain range, the Andes, on the other. Vast fields of grain and corn and prairies to graze cattle are out of the question. Fish, however, abound; almost four million metric tons of seafood per year are harvested off the coast of Chile. Fish, fruits and vegetables grown in their fertile land, and beef imported from neighboring Argentina to supplement the local herds, are featured on Chilean tables. Yet, although dominated by the culture of old Spain, much of Chilean food reflects a French influence—*meuniere* and other Gallic sauces, for example—the contribution of the French who migrated to Chile over the years.

Peru's cuisine has a Chinese twist for similar reasons; many Peruvian families have Chinese ancestors in their histories. The same is true of Cuba, whose cuisine features Chinese dishes among the Spanish specialties.

The cuisines of the world are rich with the fingerprints of time, imprinted by the cultures that have swirled around the world. A study of the fingerprints soon leads to a dim intuition of forgotten times, of aromatic mists that evoke camp-fires, feasts, and foods that bring to life long-dead cultures. They enable us to understand not only how our ancestors lived, but, with a little imagination, to smell and taste their food.

Musical instruments found in the tombs of Pharaohs made an eerie noise when played for the first time several thousand years later. The Egyptians left no notes or scores; their music will always be a mystery. But by hearing the sounds they heard, played on the very instruments they played on, it is possible to evoke the spirits of dead civilizations; to gain, however brief and incomplete, an insight into how they lived, and to understand history in a way no printed words can suggest.

So it is with food lore. What fun it is to make, from an original recipe in the cookbook of Apicius, a dish enjoyed by Romans two thousand years ago and discover that it is not only delicious, but nourishes the mind with thoughts of ancient Rome and stirs the intellect to study further. This is the romance of food.

It is time food was celebrated for the central role it plays in the civilizations of mankind. Let's hang up our aprons for a few moments, wipe the sauce from our hands, and invite food out of the kitchen and into the living room where it can tell us amazing things about itself, things that will enrich our understanding of life on earth.

It is time we had a dinner honoring food, and raised a toast to good health; for without food, nothing would exist. Let us start our search with food, the foundation of life, the engine of civilization.

Chapter 1

Food in History

The destiny of nations depends upon what and how they eat.

> *La Physiologie du Goût*
> Anthelme Brillat-Savarin

If, as Alexander Pope wrote, "the proper study of mankind is man," then the study might begin in mankind's middle, where the stomach is located. Although food has been the moving force for much of the world's history it has never received the attention it deserves, in part because past historians have not tracked the history of food nearly so carefully as that of the people who ate it.

What generals and emperors dined on is as compelling as the wars they declared. Tantalizing clues abound: Louis XIV was a glutton; Adolf Hitler was a chocoholic, as was Aztec emperor Montezuma II of Mexico; Alexander the Great was an alcoholic, as was his father, Philip of Macedonia, and many Roman emperors, such as Caligula, Claudius, Nero, and others. Ronald Reagan's fondness for sugar in the form of jellybeans is well-documented. Napolean was a gourmet, and sought out fine foods wherever his military and political adventures brought him. Former Israeli prime minister Golda Meir reportedly enchanted more than one tough visiting diplomat by serving a meal she cooked herself.

Food has always been the fuel that has driven civilization, and it has been the cause of many wars over the millennia. But it was usually the wars that were written about, not the food.

Writing today about food's place in history is akin to navigating from maps from five hundred years ago: they depict the world inaccurately and there are large areas labeled, "Terra Incognita. Here there be monsters."

Some sources contradict others. For example, the potato chip was invented either by an African-American in New Orleans or an American Indian in New York, depending on what source is consulted. The frankfurter was invented in Frankfurt, Germany . . . or was it Vienna, Austria . . . or maybe Coney Island, New York? A certain way of preparing potatoes is called french-fried because they were first made in France . . . or was it Belgium? Vichysoisse, that quintessential cold French soup, was first made in Vichy, France . . . or was it New York City? Perhaps neither is correct; perhaps both are. The telephone, radio, Polaroid, and many other inventions are believed to have been invented simultaneously by different people. Why should not the same phenomenon apply to food, with potato chips and other delights entering civilization at more than one place?

The dates listed in the timeline below are as accurate as could be determined, and the versions presented are either unquestionably accurate or the most reasonable sounding. Certain dates are approximate. For example, if something happened between 600 and 500 B.C., the earlier date is used for the sake of simplicity.

The Search for Food Begins

Homo erectus, the direct ancestor of modern *Homo sapiens,* emerged about a half-million years ago, rubbing his eyes in the sunlight. He was hungry. He caught what animals he could with his bare hands or by throwing rocks at them. Because he was an omnivore, he didn't depend on meat, but foraged for berries, roots, and the fruit of trees when he could. When he invented the spear he was able to hunt more efficiently. The search for food was considerably aided around 46,000 B.C.

when the bow and arrow appeared in Africa, and later in central Asia around 13,000 B.C.

About twelve thousand years ago, farming began in the Middle East in the vicinity of Israel, Syria, Iraq, and Iran—an area called the Fertile Crescent. The first crops grown are believed to have been the wild ancestors of wheat and barley. Villages sprang up among the farms and grew into towns, which grew into cities. It then occurred to some citizens that if they controlled enough cities they could amass wealth and power. The nation-state came into being. Pottery appeared in Japan during this period, permitting better preparation and storage of food.

About 9000 B.C., Baltic tribes invented the fishing net. Domestication of sheep began in Iraq and Roumania. The glacial tempo of agrarian progress quickened around 7000 B.C. with the domestication of pigs. Pottery appeared in the Middle East. In Mexico, the cultivation of wild squash, chili peppers, and gourds began.

Around 6500 B.C. the salt mines of Salzburg (salt-town), Austria, opened for business, in time to salt the steaks from cows, first domesticated in Turkey or Macedonia several hundred years later. In Mexico, maize (corn) was cultivated and beans appeared in Peru. Each kernel of ancestral corn was enclosed in a husk and the entire corn head was probably smaller than an ear of wheat. Farmers near sources of water were freed from the tyranny of drought when irrigation was developed around 5,000 B.C. in Khuzistan, near the Persian Gulf.

History Begins

If, as a pundit in the United States Department of State claimed, history ended in 1990, it may have begun in 4241 B.C. The Julian calendar, adopted in 46 B.C., put the number of days in the year at 365.25, introduced leap year to make up the discrepancy, and gave 4241 B.C. as the date history officially started. Rice appeared in Thailand around that time. Olives, figs, dates, grapes, and pomegranates appeared around the Mediterranean Sea. The Egyptians were busy inventing the harp and flute and their first calendar, while in nearby Babylon the Sumerians were scratching information on clay tablets and setting in place the foundations of empire. The first beer advertisement appeared in Syria, circa 4000 B.C. It was carved into a stone and read, "Drink Ebla Beer." About 3500 B.C. the Egyptians invented plowing, manuring, and raking, and farmed emmer (a primitive, starchy wheat), castor beans, grapes, barley, dates, flax, and sesame. Around 3200 B.C. it became possible for an Egyptian to say, "Hold the onions," when the lachrymose globe appeared, first in Iran and Pakistan, and quickly thereafter throughout the Mediterranean and Asia.

3000 to 2000 B.C.: Beer and Chickens

The millennium started auspiciously with the Sumerians learning to grow barley, bake bread, and brew beer. Egyptian traders brought knowledge of Egyptian farming methods to Africa and other areas. Grape wine appeared in Mesopotamia; pears in Sumer. The Chinese grew radishes and soy beans. Sugar was made from cane in India. A frieze carved about 2900 B.C. at Ur, the Sumerian city where Abraham was born, (present-day Iraq), contained the first depiction of milking. During this millennia the Sphinx of Giza and the Pyramid of Cheops were built and the Egyptians decided that their Pharaohs were gods.

Around 2700 B.C. rhubarb appeared in Asia Minor and the eastern Mediterranean, and another hundred years saw the Egyptians discovering how to leaven bread. During this period the dog was domesticated and wrestling became the first world-class spectator sport.

Approximately 2500 B.C. the Babylonians domesticated chickens. The *Farmer's Almanac* was written in Sumeria, the first guide to summarize all knowledge of how to farm. It did not include snow forecasts. Cantaloupes appeared in Iran and India circa 2400 B.C. and oranges were cultivated in China in 2200 B.C. Around this time the Egyptians made paper from papyrus and invented the first library. In Mesopotamia the potter's wheel and the kiln appeared.

2000 to 1000 B.C.: Rice and Onions

During this span of years the Egyptians wrote the first novel, *The Story of Sinuhe*. While the early Britons were building Stonehenge, the Babylonians were using advanced geometry to measure the stars. Rice cultivation began in India around the year 2000 B.C. and the horse was domesticated in Eurasia. Bananas appeared in the Indus valley; peaches were grown in China; watermelons in central Africa. Around 1900 B.C. chopsticks appeared in China.

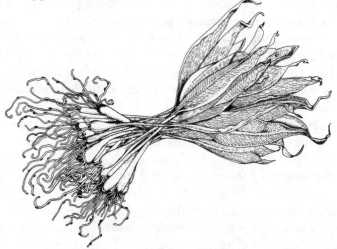

In 1550 B.C. the Codex Ebers, an Egyptian medical papyrus, advised using certain foods to cure illness, notably onions and garlic. Some Egyptians worshiped onions and swore oaths on them. Pharaoh Akenaton challenged Egyptian orthodoxy by positing that only one god existed, the god of the sun. His revolutionary ideas were reversed by King Tut. Moses led the Israelites out of Egypt. In 1300 B.C., Ramses II cultivated apples and planted orchards in the Nile delta.

1000 to 500 B.C.: Candy and Grapes

The Egyptians started the millennium sweetly by learning how to make candy from honey, nuts, spices, and seeds. The first confectioner appeared in a hieroglyphic. King David united Judah and Israel, with the capital in Jerusalem. Meanwhile, back in Babylon, the Chaldeans were busy measuring time, weight, and length using cubes filled with water. In China, mathematics leaped forward and the theory of motion was proposed. Around 800 B.C. the Chinese learned how to store ice during winter for summer use in evaporation-cooled ice houses. Then they learned how to boil beer, pour the steam back into the beer, and repeat the process until a form of hard liquor (arrack) was created (40 percent alcohol). It was now possible to put some ice in a glass of liquor and figure the odds on a bet. The only thing lacking for real gambling was money, which the Lydians of southwest Turkey obligingly invented, circa 700 B.C.

The exchange of food based on money opened worldwide opportunities. Markets expanded dramatically during the millennium: the Phoenicians migrated into Cyprus, Morocco, and the western Mediterranean; the Ionians founded twelve new cities in Asia Minor; the Greeks settled the coast of Spain; the Etruscans moved into Italy; and, in 753 B.C. the city of Rome came into being. The Greeks founded Messina and Syracuse in Sicily, the Spartans founded Taranto, Attic Greek nobles settled in Athens, and the Celts moved into Britain. The migrations were followed by countless wars, insurrections, rebellions, and destruction.

The plunder looted during the wars lined the pockets of the conquerors, but the raids and invasions also had the positive effect of spreading farming techniques, new fruits and vegetables, and cooking methods around the Mediterranean. Around 600 B.C. the Greeks brought olive trees to Italy and about 500 B.C. grapes began to be cultivated in Italy and France (ancient Gaul). Carrots were grown in Afghanistan and artichokes appeared in the central Mediterranean area.

500 B.C. to A.D. 1: Asparagus and Wine

During this period Greek art, literature, and government flowered. There were only two million Greeks, although they were attended by one million slaves. (In Athens there were 50,000 free citizens and 100,000 slaves.)

Around 400 B.C. the first food critic, Archestratus, a poet, visited all the lands in the Mediterranean area in pursuit of "delights of the belly," and returned to tell his Greek colleagues what and how to eat. Archestratus claimed to have invented *made dishes,* (the recipe). The first how-to books appeared on various types of cooking, national styles, and so on, although nothing but fragments remain today.

The Picts brewed Britain's first beer, made from heather, about 250 B.C. The workers building the Great Wall of China in 215 B.C. probably didn't get any of the Mandarin oranges, which were introduced five years earlier. Gears had recently been invented and someone created a device that would irrigate fields using gears, oxen for power, and a water wheel. The Romans learned how to pave and were busily paving their streets when asparagus appeared in the eastern Mediterranean area during this period. In 123 B.C., Gauis Gracchus, a Roman Tribune, invented the welfare state and food subsidies. Food was distributed in Rome at a discount to placate the masses.

The year 121 B.C. was a good one for wine. *Opimiam,* the first truly great wine, made its debut in Italy. This was the wine Trimalchio served to his properly impressed guests in the feast described by Petronius in *The Satyricon,* (although scholars believe that Trimalchio, the first wine snob, was cheated because the wine was mislabeled). Resin-flavored Greek wine became less popular as Italian wines took over the market.

Dioscorides, surgeon to the Roman army, used onions and garlic to cure his troops of worms. Oranges reached Rome from China, and strawberries appeared in Italy. The Roman

general Lucullus, a famed epicure, imported cherry trees from Asia Minor into Rome in 79 B.C., and the period came to an impressive gastronomic end in A.D. 1 when another Roman epicure, M. Gaius Apicius, published the first true cookbook in western civilization. It contained recipes of the time, many from his travels in search of rare and exotic foods. Apicius reputedly spent an enormous fortune in his quest for new foods.

A.D. 1 to 1000: Spinach and Coffee

Diamonds made their appearance in A.D. 16 in India, where they were prized as pretty stones, but left uncut. The Romans cleaned up their act in A.D. 50, when they learned from the Gauls how to use soap. Petronius, author of *The Satyricon,* died at his own hand in A.D. 66, but not before exposing Emperor Nero's degeneracy. The Chinese paused for a break from their inventing in the year 500 when tea came to China from India.

In 640 the Welsh army pinned leeks to their clothing before battling a British king, and won. The leeks got the credit for the victory. The leek has been a symbol of good luck for the Welsh ever since.

Spinach was cultivated in Iran in 647; sugar in Egypt in 710; and in 750 the Bavarians used hops for the first time to make beer. In 779 the Chinese published *Ch'a Ching,* a handbook about tea, and in 850 another landmark in food occurred: according to legend, Kaldi, a simple Ethiopian goatherd, discovered the coffee bean. The millennium ended as lemons appeared in north Burma and the Canary Islands.

1000 to 1500: Corn and Potatoes

Although the end of the world did not occur in the year 1000, as predicted, it became technically possible when the Chinese invented gunpowder. Potatoes and corn were planted in Peru and, in 1191, as great cathedrals rose all over Europe, tea arrived in Japan from China. In 1300 Marco Polo brought noodles back from China, European alchemists discovered how to distill alcohol, and papayas were grown in the West Indies. In 1330 halitosis became a social problem: King Alfonso XI of Castile forbade his knights to appear in court or talk with other knights for one month after they ate onions or garlic. In 1390 the master cooks of King Richard II wrote *The Forme of Cury* (The Form of Cookery), one of the earliest European cookbooks.

By 1450, the city of Mocha, in Yemen, was supplying much of the world with coffee. The first cookbook to be printed on a printing press, *Kuchenmeisterey,* (Cooking Mastery), appeared in Nuremberg in 1485 and was so popular that fifty-six editions were printed. Columbus set sail in 1492, discovered the New World, and brought strange new fruits and vegetables back to Europe, such as potatoes and pineapples. Mangoes appeared in southeast Asia.

1500 to 1600: Chocolate and Tomatoes

This Is The Boke of Cokery, the first cookbook to be printed in England, appeared in 1500. It was aimed at the households of princes and the wealthy and concentrated on the Medieval recipes and cooking techniques of the past. Despite its authoritative title, it had no real impact except as a historical first.

Pineapples became popular in Europe in 1514 and three years later the first coffee arrived in Europe, followed in 1520 by the arrival of chocolate into Spain from Mexico. South American turkeys were brought to England in 1524 and sugar cane cultivation began in Brazil in 1532. The *Book of Herbs* was published by German botanist Otto Braunfels. The works of Chaucer were published in the same year and Francisco Pizarro set out for his bloody journey to the Peru of the Incas. In 1542 Mary, Queen of Scots, ascended to the throne, Pope Paul III officially started the Inquisition in Rome, and Andrew Boorde, physician to Henry VIII, wrote *A Dietary of Helth,* advising physicians to consult cooks in preparing food for the sick.

Bavarians were reeling in their beer halls in 1542 when they learned about the government's punitive taxes on alcoholic drinks. In 1551 the pub debuted: alehouses and taverns were licensed in England and Wales. In 1568 Alexander Nowell, Dean of St. Paul's, London, invented a method of bottling beer, traditionally sold from kegs because of its effervescence. Coffee was imported from Turkey to Italy in 1580 by Venetian merchants. The Italian cooking style became all the rage in Europe. Galileo became a math professor at the University of Pisa, and forks were introduced in France.

Tomatoes arrived in England from the New World in 1596 and a year later John Gerard wrote his monumental book, *Herball,* in London, describing hundreds of food plants, many for the first time.

1600 to 1700: Tea and Ice Cream

As William Shakespeare scratched away with his quill, writing *Troilus and Cressida,* in 1601, Thomas Coryate was introducing the fork to England. Spoons and knives and bare hands were the only utensils at the time; the fork allowed a longer reach and a more secure grip on the food that was impaled. Limes appeared in the western hemisphere. In 1610 Chinese tea was shipped to Europe for the first time by the Dutch East India Company. In 1615 cookbooks in the form of guides for the housewife became popular in Europe.

Potato crops were planted in Germany in 1621. The American Indians introduced European settlers to popcorn and other new foods at the first Thanksgiving feast, in Plymouth, Massachusetts. The Kikkoman company began selling soy sauce in Japan in 1630 (still going strong in the 1990s).

In 1636 tea came to Paris, and the first cafe in Europe opened in Venice in 1640, the year Rembrandt painted his *Self Portrait*. The Saugus Iron Works in Lynn, Massachusetts, made the first cooking pot in the New World in 1642. A year later Paris discovered the pleasures of drinking coffee and the first English coffee house opened in Oxford in 1650. Tea was introduced into England the same year, as was the turnip.

Pierre Francois de la Varenne wrote *Le Cuisinièr Francois* in 1651, bringing the developing cuisine of France into a book for the first time. A major landmark in the history of food, this book broke with Medieval cuisine and the traditional methods of cooking and set the stage for the flowering, not only of French cuisine, but of all modern food preparation.

In 1652 the first coffee house in London opened in St. Michael's Alley, Cornhill. Five years later chocolate drinking was introduced to London. Samuel Pepys told his diary about "*tee,* a drink of which I never had drank before."

Isaac Newton measured the orbit of the moon in 1666, the same year cheddar cheese was invented in Cheddar, England. Haute cuisine's first (and last, to date) martyr had his fifteen minutes of fame in 1676. The famed chef Vatel (Le Grande) was to cook a fish dinner for Louis XIV. The fish didn't arrive in time and Vatel committed suicide. The same chef may have been the first to serve ice cream in France. He made a frozen sweetmeat in the shape of an egg and served it to Louis and his guests. A year later Paris went crazy over ice cream; it became France's most popular dessert.

Two years later the French inventor Denis Papin created the pressure cooker. The first Viennese coffee house opened in 1683. Croissants were invented in Austria that year. Viennese bakers made the celebratory bun in a crescent shape, a *croissant,* to resemble the flag of Turkey, in commemoration of their holding off the attack by Ottoman Turks early that year. When

a Viennese ate a croissant, he was eating the flag of Turkey. The Cafe Procope opened in Paris in 1686 and was an immediate success. In 1698 Mrs. White's Chocolate House opened in London and became Tory headquarters, as well as England's first private club.

1700 to 1800: Sugar Beets and Gin

Twining's of London, tea merchants, opened for business in 1706. The event may possibly have been noted in *The Evening Post,* the first evening paper ever published, which began its circulation the same year. In 1724 gin drinking became popular and its use, and abuse, began to spread in England.

Coffee was planted in Brazil in 1727 for the first time. In 1739, *Les Dons De Comus,* by Francois Marin, the first cookbook for the common person, appeared in France. It explained to the uninitiated not only how to prepare a fine dinner but also how to *serve* it with elegance and style. Three years later the first American cookbook, Eliza Smith's *The Compleat Housewife* was published, and in 1746 *La Cuisinière Bourgeoisie* by Menon appeared, a four-hundred-page cookbook for the lower middle classes with recipes for cooking inferior cuts of meat and other hints on how to eat well inexpensively. It became a best-seller as the masses scrambled to learn how to cook.

In 1747 sugar was discovered in beets by a German chemist, A.S. Marggraf. Baker's chocolate plant opened in Dorchester, Mass., in 1765. It is the oldest food company in the United States and the first to make chocolate in the New World. Potatoes became Europe's most popular food.

The year of the Boston Massacre, 1770, was also the year in which the source of the Blue Nile was discovered, and the year Captain Cook discovered Australia. Handel's *Messiah* was performed in New York, the painters Tiepolo and Boucher died, Gainsborough painted *Blue Boy,* and Mrs. van Beethoven gave birth to a boy she named Ludwig. In Paris, a chef, M. Boulanger, made culinary history when he opened the world's first true restaurant. Two years later, Georg Lahner was born in Germany and was destined to contribute to American cuisine in a major way: he is credited with the invention of the frankfurter.

In 1773, as the waltz craze swept Vienna, Britain imposed a discriminatory tax on tea in the American colonies, leading to the Boston Tea Party. Jethro Tull's seed planting machine was perfected in 1782, resulting in larger harvests and less wasted seed. Six years later the first porcelain-coated metal pots were manufactured by Konigsbronn foundry in Wurttemberg. Although the porcelain was pure white, it didn't stain, was easy to clean, and food didn't stick to the inside walls, a major advance in kitchen technology.

In 1789 the mobs of the French Revolution stormed the Bastille, the first U. S. Congress met, the mutineers from The H. M. S. *Bounty* landed on Pitcairn Island, and Count Rumford, the founder of domestic science, built the first scientifically-constructed kitchen range, ending the centuries-old domination of fireplace cooking. A year later Thomas Harris and John Long patented a refrigeration machine in Great Britain.

1800 to 1850: The Tin Can and Macadamia Nuts

In 1801, at the urging of Napoleon, a sugar-beet refining plant was built in Silesia. (France became self-sufficient in sugar by 1840, with fifty-eight factories; Germany and Belgium shortly followed suit.) In 1803 Henry Shrapnel invented a deadly artillery shell, Robert Fulton invented the steam boat, and Thomas Moore invented the insulated ice box. Benjamin Stillman began selling bottled soda water at his store in Yale University in 1807. Two years later Joseph Hawkins of Philadelphia patented an efficient process of carbonation.

Nicholas Appert, a Frenchman, entered a contest held by Napoleon in 1810 to find a better way to get food to troops at the front, and won with his invention: bottled food. Two years later, while Napoleon retreated from the Russian campaign after losing over a half-million soldiers, Brian Donkin, an Englishman, invented the tin can.

The first shot in the drive for pure food was fired in 1820 with the publication of Frederick Accum's *Treatise on The Adulteration of Food, and Culinary Poisons* in England.

Gregor Mendel was born in 1822. The Austrian monk's experiments with breeding peas in the priory garden led to the selective breeding of plants and animals with superior qualities and laid the foundation for the genetic engineering of food.

In 1825 Anthelme Brillat-Savarin wrote his cuisine classic, *La Physiologie de Goût*. British chemist John Walker invented the friction match in 1826, making it easy to light kitchen fires, as well as lamps. The year 1830 was good for food: as new-fangled steam automobiles chugged around London, Dr. J. G. B. Siegert began bottling aromatic bitters under the name Angostura; William Alcott opened the first store specializing in health foods in Boston; French-style restaurants became popular in London (ladies were not welcomed); and the Jamaican grapefruit was recognized by botanists as a genuinely new fruit.

Cyrus McCormick patented the reaping machine in 1834, ending the hand-harvesting of grains with scythes, a method in use since the beginning of agriculture. It was now possible for a few farm hands with one machine to harvest in a few days what formerly took hundreds of people weeks to do. The mechanical thresher was introduced by Pitts three years later. It separated the grain from the chaff, the external envelope of each grain, mechanically, instead of manually by beating handfuls of grain-laden stalks against an object, and did for threshing what the reaper did for harvesting.

These mechanical inventions, and others which followed, revolutionized agriculture and made it possible for a few people to farm vast fields in a short time. The principles of artificial fertilizers were discovered by Liebig in 1840. Steel rollers replaced stones in the grinding of wheat that year, making the removal of the germ (the heart of the grain kernel) much easier. Wheat germ and oil were removed and fed to poultry and livestock and the remaining grain was used to make white bread. A traditional symbol of affluence, white bread became popular across the United States.

Potato rot caused monumental crop failures in Europe in 1845, and a famine began in Ireland. Queen Victoria's head chef, Charles Edme Francatelli, wrote a cookbook, *The Modern Cook,* with recipes for humble cuts of meat (sheep's ears) as well as exotic items (reindeer tongue). The next year, *Mrs Beecher's Domestic Receipt Book* was published in the United States. It was among the first cookbooks to include detailed recipes for dishes and specific directions for food preparation. The instructions given in previous cookbooks were rather vague, such as "take some beef and cook it until done."

Evaporated milk was invented in 1847, the year Marx and Engels issued *The Communist Manifesto,* and Auguste Escoffier, one of history's greatest chefs, was born. During this era Alexandre Dumas wrote his *Dictionary of Cuisine* and popularized the quest for gourmet food at his weekly dinners.

The safety match was invented by Bottger in 1848, and the first macaroni factory in the United States opened for business in Brooklyn, New York. R. W. Bunsen invented the gas burner in 1850. Techniques for bottling beer had been invented earlier, but bottled beer didn't become popular until the 1850s, when large-scale breweries began appearing in the United States. The Macadamia nut was discovered by Ferdinand von Meuller.

1850 to 1900: Margarine and Soft Drinks

Isaac Singer invented the sewing machine, Herman Melville wrote *Moby Dick,* the *New York Times* debuted, and the consumption of liquor was banned in Maine, Illinois in 1851. Emigration from Ireland as a result of the potato famine reached 250,000 per year.

Alexis Soyer, chef at the prestigious Reform Club in England, published a best-seller, *A Shilling Cookery For The People,* in 1855. It was aimed at lower class households and sold 250,000 copies. The next year saw the Borden's Company introducing condensed milk. Diamond Jim Brady, whose eating habits gave new meaning to the word *glutton,* was born.

In 1857 Louis Pasteur proved that fermentation is caused by living organisms. The Great Atlantic and Pacific Tea Company was founded in 1859, and opened the first A & P grocery store in New York City in 1869—the first modern chain store. In 1860 the first pure food and drug act became law in Great Britain, the same year that H.J. Heinz started off his fifty-seven varieties by selling dried, canned horseradish in Pittsburgh.

In 1861 Agoston Haraszthy imported 100,000 vines of three hundred different varieties of grape to California and became the father of the California wine industry. In Australia, the first cold storage unit operated by machine was built by T. S. Mort. The landmark *Book of Household Management,* by Isabella Beeton was published in England. It was the first cookbook to include the cost of ingredients, length of time to cook dishes, and quantity of each ingredient. The Confederates took Fort Sumter. The population of the United States was thirty-two million.

The following year Victor Hugo wrote *Les Misérables,* the Red Cross was founded, Lincoln freed the slaves, and German scientist Julius Sachs proved starch is produced by plant photosynthesis. Obesity was recognized as a health problem in 1863 with the publication of *Letter On Corpulence* by British cabinet-maker William Banting. It contained the first slimming diet, *The Banting System.*

The first salmon cannery built in the United States (at Washington, California) began operations in 1864. Louis Pas-

teur invented pasteurization and pasteurized wine. The following year Domingo Ghirardelli made ground chocolate in San Francisco, Thaddeus Lowe invented a machine to make ice, Dr. Caleb Jackson invented an early version of granola, and Chicago opened its first stockyard that, with the expansion of the railroads, began bringing fresh meat to the entire country. The first train robbery took place in North Bend, Ohio. The Civil War ended; the Boer War began.

In 1868 the oldest food trademark in the United States hit the market when canned Underwood Deviled Ham began sales; tabasco sauce was marketed; P. D. Armour opened the first meat-packing plant in Chicago; and John Deere patented a revolutionary steel plow and opened a factory to make them. Handmade tin cans became obsolete with the introduction of a machine that manufactured them automatically. This was also the year when the first pro baseball team, the Cincinnati Red Stockings, was formed, the management immediately putting all players in uniform (with red stockings).

Fish-and-chips shops appeared in England in 1870. They proved a boon to the working class by making protein and vitamin C (from potatoes) widely available and cheap. American inventor William Lyman patented the first practical can-opener. The following year chefs at the Palace Hotel in San Francisco invented Green Goddess salad dressing and Oysters Kirkpatrick, and popularized a strange new vegetable, the artichoke. Alexander Graham Bell invented the telephone in 1876, setting the stage for home delivery of pizza less than a hundred years later.

The first refrigerated railroad cars left Chicago in 1877 with a load of fresh meat. The first frozen meat arrived in Europe from Argentina. Margarine, an idea dreamed up by Emperor Napoleon III, began to be mass-produced in America under the name *butterine*. A mechanical cream separator was invented by Gustav de Laval, and a year later an American, John Francis Appleby, invented a machine to bind and knot grain sheaves. He is more famous for his deadlier inventions: an automatic feed device for rifles as well as the cartridge magazine. Scotland Yard was established in London, whose streets glowed with electric lights for the first time.

The first refrigerated ship, the British freighter *Strathleven,* began hauling meat from Australia and New Zealand to England in 1879. Frozen meat was sold in London. Saccharin was discovered by Fahlberg and Remser. Joseph Stalin, Leon Trotsky, Paul Klee, Albert Einstein, and E. M. Forster were born. The following year Civil War hero Lew Wallace wrote *Ben Hur* in Santa Fe, Gilbert and Sullivan wrote *The Pirates of Penzance,* Edison invented the electric light (and so did J. W. Swan, independently of each other), Bingo was developed from an old Italian game called *tumbula,* and canned meat and fruit were sold in stores for the first time.

In 1883, the Brooklyn Bridge opened, the Orient Express began its run, and Buffalo Bill enchanted easterners with his Wild West Show. A Civil War veteran named Charles Stillwell, who tinkered with machines in his backyard to pass the time, invented an ingenious device that made paper bags automatically. Because of the Cuban war with Spain, a Cuban customer could not pay his American miller's bill in 1885. He sent coconuts instead and Baker's Coconut entered the American market.

A year later, Dr. John Pemberton, an Atlanta druggist, invented a soothing cough syrup. An employee put some in carbonated water and Coca-Cola was born. Dr. Pepper and Hire's Root Beer were created the same year. Aluminum cookware was invented by Charles Martin Hall in Ohio, but didn't catch on until Wanamaker's department store in New York held public demonstrations of Hall's Wear-Ever pots in 1903. Josephine Cochrane, a society matron in Illinois, invented a machine to wash dishes. Her device became the Kitchenaid dishwasher. Nicola Tesla invented the electric motor in 1888; George Westinghouse built it and sold it to the public.

In the United States the era of the free lunch began in 1890. A five-cent mug of beer at a saloon entitled one to construct his lunch from a modest buffet at no extra charge (no women permitted). Tea rooms for the ladies gained popularity in the United States, and many restaurants began to serve both ladies and gentlemen. Lipton's Tea entered the market.

The first electric stove was exhibited in London in 1891; canned pineapple appeared the following year. Joshua Pusey of Lima, Pennsylvania, invented the matchbook, and British physicist Sir James Dewar invented the thermos bottle.

In 1893 the first completely electric kitchen went on display at the Chicago World's Fair, featuring a range, broiler, and tea-kettles. In 1894 Milton Hershey discovered how to make a bar of chocolate and began selling Hershey Bars. Fannie Farmer's *Boston Cook Book* was published in 1896. It was the first cookbook to standardize measurements, removing the guesswork from the preparation of dishes. Leonard Hershfield made a chewy candy roll that year and named it after his daughter, Tootsie. Two years before the end of the century Pepsi-Cola entered the market.

1900 to 1925: Hot Dogs and Sliced Bread

In 1900 Americans did the Cake Walk, and hungered for something to eat with their Pepsis, Cokes, and Dr. Peppers. Food vendor Harry Stevens obliged by putting a frankfurter on a bun at the Polo Grounds in New York during a Giants baseball game. The hot dog was an immediate success and became wildly popular. In 1902 Jell-O was introduced via the first national food advertising campaign. On June 2, Joe Horn and Frank Hardart opened Horn & Hardart's, the first automated restaurant, a fast-food precursor.

"I'm drinking Canada Dry," became the gag in 1904 when the new ginger ale entered the market. The Pure Food and Drug Act became law in the United States in 1906; Upton Sinclair's book *The Jungle* was given credit for motivating Congress to pass it. Mrs. Melitta Bentz in Germany invented a simple way of making coffee the following year. Soybeans were planted in England in 1908. Hugh Moore invented the disposable paper cup. (In 1919 the same inventor introduced the Dixie Cup.)

California cuisine debuted in 1910 when the St. Francis Hotel (San Francisco) chef Victor Hirtzler, formerly chef for King Don Carlos of Portugal, published *The St. Francis Cookbook*. Cellophane was invented in 1912 by Edwin Bradenburger. Kasimir Funk coined the word *vitamin*. In 1915 the first automotive tractor was made by Henry Ford. Heat-resistant Pyrex glass was invented at the Corning Glass Works in Pennsylvania. Food rationing was implemented in Germany in 1916 by Walther Rathenau, Germany's Economic Director, to counter the Allied blockade during World War I. Delivery boy Nathan Handwerker opened a hot dog stand on Coney Island and called it Nathan's.

As World War I raged through Europe in 1917, and women were being jailed for picketing the White House for the right to vote, Ed Cox of San Francisco invented a pre-soaped pad to clean pots with; his wife named it S.O.S. (Save Our

Saucepans). Two years later mechanic Charles Strite invented the pop-up toaster.

In 1920 Mexican aerialist Alfredo Codona became the first person to do a triple somersault, and the Volstead Act ushered in prohibition (which lasted until 1930). The tea bag was invented in San Francisco by J. Krieger, and the first bread slicer was marketed. With the growth of international highways, Californians created the drive-in restaurant. Fictional spokesperson Betty Crocker was created in 1921; table tennis became a national craze, Sacco and Vanzetti were found guilty of murder, and the British Broadcasting Company was founded. In Switzerland, Doctor Bircher-Benner wrote *The Fundaments of Our Nutrition,* advocating the eating of raw food. Peter Paul Halijian made a candy bar of coconut covered with bittersweet chocolate and called it Mounds. (In 1947 he topped each Mound with an almond and dubbed the confection an Almond Joy.) Another candy-maker, Otto Schnering, dreamed up a candy bar made from fudge, chocolate, peanuts, and caramel and named it after President Grover Cleveland's daughter, Baby Ruth Cleveland. While touring a teakettle factory on a trip to Germany, American Joseph Block got a bright idea, went home, and invented the whistling teakettle.

As America was gripped by candy-mania, one of the pioneers of the industry, George Cadbury, died in England in 1922. An American invention, the cocktail, swept Europe. Stephen Poplawski invented a food blender, later redesigned and financed by musician Fred Waring. The water-softener was invented in 1924 by Emmett Culligan, in St. Paul, Minnesota.

1925 to 1950: Frozen Foods and Microwave Ovens

In 1925, as skirts went above the knees, cloche hats became popular, and the nation did the Charleston, Clarence Birdseye was inventing a method of quick-freezing food. In 1927 Alex

Cardini invented the Caesar Salad in Tijuana, Mexico. Brazil's economy collapsed a year later as the nation overproduced coffee. A fish-deboning machine was invented in England.

The first supermarket, a self-service grocery store, opened in Jamaica, New York in 1930. Candy-maker Franklin Mars debuted Snickers, an immediate hit with the public. After six tries, 7-Up was born in 1933. A printing salesman sent his pals a list of his favorite restaurants instead of a Christmas card in 1935; The Duncan Hines restaurant and hotel guides were born. Kreuger, the first canned beer, was made in New Jersey. Sylvan Goldman, a grocer in Oklahoma City, took pity on his customers in 1936 and invented the shopping cart. Two years later, Dr. Roy Plunkett, a chemist for DuPont, invented tetra-fluoroethylene, known as Teflon. In 1954 a French company began making pots coated with it, but it was not until 1960 that an American store, Macy's, stocked them. They were an immediate hit.

World War II was gathering momentum in Europe in 1939, as Americans thrilled to the Technicolor wonders of *The Wizard of Oz.* DDT, first discovered in 1874, was hailed as a wonder-chemical for agriculture and people: malaria was wiped out in Sri Lanka and British Guiana with it. In 1940, Howard Florey developed penicillin, and James Beard published the first of his many food books, *Hors d'Oeuvres and Canapes.* Innovative Mars, Inc. devised a candy for war-bound G.I.s, *M & M's,* that "melt in your mouth, not in your hand." The Chemex coffee-maker was invented by a German immigrant to the United States, Dr. Peter Schlumbohm.

In 1945, Earl Tupper, a chemist for DuPont, fashioned a tumbler of polyethylene and started a party that is still going on: Tupperware revolutionized the kitchen container industry and made Tupper a multi-millionaire. The following year, as the Iron Curtain fell over Eastern Europe, a Raytheon Company employee, Percy Spencer, accidentally melted some chocolate with microwaves. The first microwave oven was marketed one year later.

Pillsbury and General Mills introduced the first cake mixes in 1947. Al Capone died, Jackie Robinson broke the color barrier in baseball, the Dead Sea Scrolls were discovered in Israel, and Richard Reynolds invented aluminum foil.

1950 to the 1990s: Convenience and Consumerism

Americans were singing a song about food, "If I Knew You Were Comin' I'd've Baked A Cake," as the fifties opened. The population of the United States was at an all-time high of 150,697,999, and there were 2.3 billion people in the entire world. Technology developed in the World War II effort was turned to consumer needs. Convenience food, non-stick pans, the TV dinner, pie-crust mixes, packaged dry soup, and bottled sauces were introduced. In 1955 the first McDonald's restaurant operated by Ray Croc opened in Des Plaines, Illinois. In 1960 the aluminum can appeared, replacing steel cans.

The Food and Agriculture Organization of the United Nations recognized hunger as a world problem in 1961, and launched the first world campaign against hunger. In 1962, Diet-Rite soda appeared, and the following year marked the premiere of the first cooking show for a national television audience as Julia Child began "The French Chef." Alcoa introduced the pull-tab top for aluminum cans, eliminating the need for can-openers. In 1965 Diet Pepsi entered the market.

Consumer spending on alcoholic beverages in the United States topped $17 billion in 1966. Four years later cyclamate artificial sweeteners were banned in the United States and Canada.

Carl Sontheimer, a retired physicist, imported the first Cuisinart from France in 1973, and in 1974 the first supermarket checkout scanner was introduced. The first item scanned was a pack of chewing gum. In 1979 the California Legislature introduced legislation to define and set standards

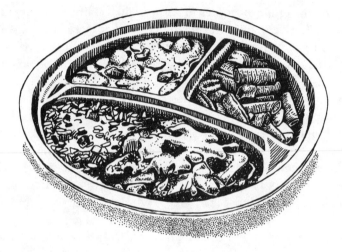

for organic farming and organic food labeling. At East Texas State University Moses Attrep, Jr. discovered prostaglandin A in onions, a chemical that lowers blood pressure.

During the 1980s the consumer movement became politicized. Celebrities lobbied against alar and Caesar Chavez continued his campaign against grape growers. Philip Sokolof spent three million dollars of his own money to get Nabisco, McDonald's, and others to stop using highly-saturated tropical oils in their products and to substitute healthier ingredients. He also instituted nation-wide programs to test people for cholesterol levels. Recycling gathered momentum.

In the 1990s the environment, food additives, and other political issues promise to remain in the forefront. Recycling and conservation of resources will become a way of life. The genetic engineering of food will continue, and the farming of fish will become routine, offering a reliable supply of untainted, fresh fish to the public. *Nouvelle cuisine* will cease to be *nouvelle* and will become the norm, as consumers continue to demand fresh, innovative, and healthy food.

As the public becomes more informed about the dangers of food additives, chemical fertilizers and insecticides, and the harm to the environment done by convenience food packaging, the demand for pure, wholesome food can be expected to increase. This pressure, expressed at the check-out counter and the voting booth, will undoubtedly result in improvements in food purity, quality, and taste. The fresh tastes of vine- and field-ripened fruits and vegetables will become increasingly available at the corner store. This growing market demand for wholesomeness and flavor can be expected to influence the way food is grown, packaged, and shipped, and may result in an increase in farms whose specialty is wholesome, flavorful foods, rushed to the table with a minimum of storage and handling.

Factory farms and manufactured foods will not disappear—if anything, their volume will increase as populations grow. But for those concerned with providing healthful foods to their families, and for those who love to cook and eat—for whom food is an adventure in creativity and pleasure—the 1990s should bring some wonderful surprises. What the future holds in store cannot be spelled out in great detail; but it will be fun to stop and eat the flowers along the way.

Chapter 2

Words for Food

A man who is careful with his palate is not likely to be careless with his paragraphs.

Clifton Fadiman

The English language is marinated in food words; words that describe food and its qualities and also serve as reliable metaphors and similes when other words fail. How many breathless poets and tongue-tied lovers have compared the lips of their beloved to cherries, their cheeks to peaches? How many call their beloved honey, or sugar, to express tenderness or curry favor? How many babies are the apple of their parents' eyes, who regularly bring home the bacon, to provide a nest egg for their brood? How many people feel sheepish if they do something wrong, and have to eat humble pie in atonement?

It's no baloney; if you want to be the top banana or be considered a big cheese, never clam up when challenged by a crab with a bitter remark, no matter how corny. Instead, it may be fruitful to cream the turkey, make mincemeat out of him, or eat him for breakfast; he's probably a nut anyhow, with a brain the size of a pea. Certainly his approach is piggish and ham-handed, but he's a chicken deep down; his knees will turn to jelly if you challenge him. Ignore the rhubarb, and milk the opportunity. He may relish a fight, but a sage and salty remark can sometimes squash that peppery shrimp's zest for argument.

Phrases such as *the busy season, a trenchant remark,* and many more, all have roots in food. From the time the first caveman grunted in appreciation as he came upon a berry-laden bush, we have been searching for the right word to describe and

35

classify each fruit, each vegetable, and each food animal. The search for food builds a strong appetite for words to describe them, and the words themselves become capable of stimulating the appetite by bringing forth fragrant, delicious images.

Salt and alcohol, two of the oldest stimulants to the appetite, are responsible for many of the food words and metaphors that have worked themselves into the language. It is appropriate to begin a journey into the world of food words with these two puzzling substances.

Salt: The Seasoning We Love and Hate

Sir Humphrey Davy
Abominated gravy.
He lived in the odium
Of having discovered sodium.

The doggerel quoted above is the very first clerihew, a form of humorous verse invented by Edmund Clerihew Bentley, a sixteen-year-old student. Bentley was damning with faint praise the discovery, in 1810, by Humphrey Davy, (1778–1829), that salt was composed of two deadly poisons, chlorine gas and sodium—a dangerously unstable liquid metal. It was his way of humorously expressing the unmasking of a mystery.

Salt has always been a puzzle, and often associated with magic. Because salt is pure (good), spilling it brought bad luck. The Devil hated salt, so all you had to do was throw some of the spilled salt into his face (he could be found over your left shoulder), and all would be well again. In some cultures salt is sprinkled on the threshold of new homes and in the corners to rid the premises of the Devil. Roman Catholics once put salt on the baby's tongue as part of the baptism rite.

When put into food it disappears completely, yet dissolved salt can be turned back into its original form by evaporation. Salt will preserve delicate food, yet destroy solid metal. Salt is a rock, not a plant, yet it can alter the taste of food more power-fully than any organic herb or spice. Although we need only a touch of salt, everyone craves it, and we are well-endowed with special taste buds on the tongue reserved only for salt. An inferior dish can be made appealing by salting it. Thirty-four percent of Americans salt their food before they even taste it.

We would die without the three-and-a-half ounces of salt our bodies contain. Some people risk death by overdosing on salt, the primary stimulus of high blood pressure. If we lose too much body salt from heavy perspiration we faint. If we eat the equivalent of an ounce of salt a day, according to one source, we can shorten our lives by thirty years. A favored way of committing suicide in ancient China was to eat a pound of salt.

A character in a Sholem Aleichem story asked the wise rabbi why the sea is salty. "Because," the rabbi pontificated, "there are so many herrings in it." No one knows precisely why the ocean is so salty (3.5 percent on average), but if all the salt in the oceans of the world were miraculously extracted it would cover the land of the earth to a depth of fourteen inches. Despite the rarity and value of salt throughout history, the earth contains salt in enormous quantities and spread around the world. When salt mines were dug in the past, an un-welcome nuisance was the black oil that often accompanied the digging. The first oil gusher, Spindletop in Texas, was drilled on the site of a large salt dome.

For every one hundred pounds of salt produced each year, only five go into your salt shaker or prepared food products. The rest is used for packing meat, feeding livestock, building roads and keeping them free of ice in winter, tanning leather, and the manufacture of glass, soaps, and other industrial uses.

When we *sal*ute someone, we hope our gesture has a *salu*-tary effect on them, and that they will somehow find *sal*vation. When we think of a delicious *sal*ami, or a *sal*ad, we *sal*ivate. These words pay tribute to the role of salt in history. The Bible mentions it more than thirty times, most famously in the tale of Mrs. Lot, whose curiosity turned her into a pillar of salt. Salt was so important in imperial Rome that soldiers were paid with it or given money to buy it: a *sala*ry. A laggard legionnaire was not worth his salt.

Salzburg, Austria, ("salt town"), is the site of one of the oldest salt mines in the world, worked by the Neolithic, or New Stone Age, culture, about 10,000 years ago. So many prehistoric bodies and tools are preserved in the salt that it is a major archaeological site and tourist attraction. Nearby is another village, whose name, Hallstat, also means salt town. Hallstat's salt mines provided so much wealth to their ancient owners that Greeks, Egyptians, and Roman traders came from all over the Mediterranean to buy salt. These ancient salt miners were Celts, whose influence spread over much of Europe as their salt salesmen traveled around.

Alcohol and Alchemy

Alcohol and alchemy are only a few definitions apart in the dictionary. Early alchemists were religious men, some of them monks, who believed they would reach god through the study of natural processes based upon distillation. The process would, they thought, distill and purify the soul to a state of spiritual perfection. To do that they needed a magical substance they dubbed the Philosopher's Stone. If they could create it in their laboratories, they thought, it would turn base metals into gold. Taken internally by a human, the Philosopher's Stone would erase age, cure diseases, and make the person who drank it immortal. It was the Medieval version of the ambrosia of Greek mythology, the food of the gods which conferred immortality on any mortal fortunate enough to eat of it.

The mother of all alchemists may have been Cleopatra, who was said to have tried to turn base metals into gold. The father of alchemy was undoubtedly a man named Jabir, who lived in Baghdad, (A.D. 721–776) and invented the still in his efforts to make gold. Using Jabir's still, other Arab alchemists distilled the essences of flowers, leaves, and grasses. Early perfumes and food flavors such as rose water developed from their experiments.

As alchemy developed, stills became more complex until, somewhere in the twelfth or thirteenth centuries, unknown European alchemists learned how to distill pure alcohol. They removed the water from wine and ale in a still, and kept redistilling the liquid until they got to an irreducible essence, which they called the spirit of the liquid: "the spirit of life," or the "water of life"; *aqua vitae.* Liquors are referred to as spirits from the alchemist's nomenclature. The word *whiskey* comes from the Irish word *uisgebeatha,* meaning "water of life," as does the Scandinavian word, *aquavit.* Whiskey, as well as a long list of modern liquors, was developed using the distillation techniques first invented by alchemists.

Alcohol has always been a provocative substance. Civilizations and their religions have usually embraced it eagerly, starting with the Babylonians and Egyptians, who liked their daily beer. The Greeks and Romans had special gods in charge of wine: Dionysus for the Greeks, and Bacchus for the Romans. Wine is an important part of Christian ritual, and Jews have always used wine in Passover as well as other religious services.

Moslems, on the other hand, forbid alcoholic consumption. Even today, in Pakistan, possession of a can of beer is sufficient cause for public flogging. The ambivalence of society towards alcohol is perhaps best symbolized by the story of Noah, considered in the Old Testament to have been the first drunk, yet celebrated as the person who built the Ark and saved the animals from extinction.

The Egyptian god Osiris was loved because he was the first to make wine and beer. He was also feared as the god of the dead, and presided over the Court of Death, which judged who would go to the next world and who would not. Today we feel pity and horror when confronted with a hopeless drunk; yet comedians reduce us to helpless laughter with hilarious imitations of such unfortunates. The ambivalence continues.

Although the ancient Greeks loved their wine, they were generally moderate in its consumption. Drunkenness was uncommon, at least in the beginning of their civilization. They used alcohol in much the same way it is used today: as part of religious rituals, as a beverage served at social functions to put the guests in a proper mood, as a medicine, and as part of the daily meal to aid digestion.

From 753 B.C., when Rome was founded, until the third century B.C., the Romans were moderate in their consumption of alcohol. The early citizens had more important things to do than drink wine. Vineyards were small and the wine produced was inferior. When the Romans conquered Italy and the rest of the Mediterranean, drinking became more widespread, the quality of wine was improved, and alcoholism became a problem.

In 586 B.C. the Hebrews were captured by the Babylonians and brought to Babylon as slaves. The Babylonians' love of drunkenness (for which they had a formidable reputation) may have contributed to the downfall of their empire in 539 B.C. The Persian army, under Cyrus, waited until the Babylonians threw a party, (the celebrated feast of Belshazzar). When the Babylonians were thoroughly drunk the attack began. It resulted in the destruction of an empire and the freeing of the Jews from captivity. The lesson was not lost on the Jews, who have a history of alcoholic moderation. "Be not drunk with wine," the Talmud admonishes, "for wine turneth the mind from the truth, and inspires the passion of lust, and leadeth the eyes into error . . ."

Alexander the Great (356 to 323 B.C.) was a notorious drunkard, a brilliant Greek general who learned how to hold his liquor from his father, King Philip of Macedonia. Alexander's fondness for drink is thought to have contributed to his early death at the age of thirty-three.

Drinking began to get out of hand around 7 B.C. in Greece. The authorities tried to combat the tendency towards drunkenness by confining large-scale consumption to government-sponsored drinking holidays. What they accomplished was to associate the drinking of alcohol with festivities, a bond that became deeply ingrained in most societies and remains so to the present day.

By the first century B.C. viticulture was a major source of revenue for the Romans and wine was popular all over the empire. Heavy drinking was encouraged by the government. It became a daily habit for almost everyone.

Medieval monks carried on the tippling tradition, although under less deadly circumstances. Writers in those days portrayed monks as hard drinkers who loved a good time—role models used by Chaucer and typified by the character of Friar Tuck in the Robin Hood stories. The monks worked assiduously at perfecting brewing and distillation processes, developing fine wines and liqueurs, and perfecting the making of champagne when they innovated the bottle cork, allowing them to use the second fermentation and to age wines in bottles. A monastic name on a bottle today is still a sign of the highest quality.

The association of alcohol with religious orders gave society the idea that drinking was a good thing. Jesus turned the water into wine in a celebrated miracle; wine represents the blood of Christ in Christian rituals; and the fact that men of God, the monks, were entrusted with the responsibility of making wine and other alcoholic beverages, sent an unmistakable message that drinking alcohol was socially acceptable. A Medieval French professor of medicine, Arnaud de Villeneuve, recommended getting drunk twice a month to rid the body of "noxious humors."

With such precedents, the tavern, favored by the Greeks and Romans, was revived and became the most important social meeting place in Medieval times. One could go to a tavern to meet old friends, eat and drink, sing drinking songs with the local minstrel, and get drunk in a socially acceptable manner.

The Irish adopted whiskey (*uisgebeatha*) as a tonic, and used it to cure hangovers. They celebrated the joy of life and eased the pain of death by introducing heavy drinking at christenings and wakes.

Alcohol was the biggest recreational sport in the early American west, and it was in the saloons that much business was transacted and decisions were made. Americans have continued the use, and abuse, of alcohol into the present. Society has often rebelled, and there were several temperance movements that led to partial banning of alcoholic beverages by some states, culminating in the Volstead Act in 1919, which ushered in prohibition as the United States prepared to enter the war in Europe. Nevertheless, people wanted their booze. Illegal saloons called speakeasys were society's answer (you had to "speak easy" to get in). Hundreds of ways were devised to hide flasks of liquor: under garters, in false books, even in the hollow heels of specially-made shoes. It was a game to many; some people made liquor in their homes (bathtub gin).

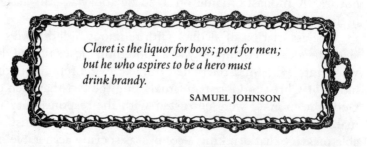

Claret is the liquor for boys; port for men; but he who aspires to be a hero must drink brandy.

SAMUEL JOHNSON

After five thousand years of drinking, the association of alcohol with life and death, happiness and misery, and solitude and companionship has become deeply ingrained in most societies. Efforts to ban alcohol consumption have failed in democratic societies and only seem to work when enforced by authoritarian rulers. Total freedom has also failed, but no government has yet found a middle way that is workable. Peo-

ple still celebrate their joys with a glass of wine, while others
drown their sorrows in it.

SOME FACTS ABOUT ALCOHOL

- The flush one feels after having a drink is caused by the
  expansion of capillaries near the surface of the skin.
  Alcohol actually lowers the body temperature.
- The martini holds the lead as America's most popular
  cocktail. Next in the mixed-drink lineup is the whiskey
  sour, followed by the bloody Mary, the Manhattan,
  the Collins, screwdriver, old-fashioned, and the gin
  and tonic.
- The Japanese produce a potent liquor by mashing
  mamushis snakes (related to the copperhead rattler) and
  fermenting and aging the runoff. Some of this liquor is
  sold with a dead snake in each bottle.
- In 1637, according to Governor Wilhelm Keift, one
  quarter of all the shops in New York were taverns.
- Today bars are forbidden near schools and churches in
  many states, but at one time in America the law stated
  that a tavern must be sited near those establishments for
  the convenience of the citizenry.

Great Wine

Pull the cork from a bottle of wine and you let a genie out that
has given pleasure to much of the world since humans first
tasted grapes. The story of wine encompasses most of history,
and is drawn from every corner of the world and every economic level of society. It embraces agriculture, science, history, commerce, art, literature, and legend.

Some of the facts of modern wine production boggle the
mind. The world's largest winery is E. & J. Gallo in Modesto,

California, with a capacity of 175 million gallons. From the window of a small plane flying over the plant it appears to be a vast oil refinery. Huge stainless steel tanks cover acres of land in serried ranks; the largest tank contains one million gallons of wine. The main warehouse covers twenty-five acres and holds only four weeks worth of stock. The largest glass factory west of the Mississippi River is on the premises.

This gargantuan factory sits in the northern third of the San Joaquin Valley, four hundred miles long and one hundred miles wide, one of the richest wine-producing regions on earth. As Hugh Johnson puts it in his book, *The World Atlas of Wine,* "If all America's wine filled one bottle, all but one-and-a-bit glasses of it would come from this giant vineyard."

One out of every one hundred people in the world either grows wine grapes, makes wine, or sells wine. The twenty-five million cultivated acres of vineyards around the world represent one acre out of every 130 acres that are cultivated worldwide, and are capable of providing every human being on earth with eight bottles of wine each year.

Because grapes can be grown and wine made in most of the world's temperate zones, unusual situations exist in some countries. In Morocco, Algeria, Tunisia, and Libya, Moslems who will not drink a drop of wine earn their livelihoods growing and bottling wine, much of it of high quality. Turkey has the fifth largest vineyard acreage in the world, but only three percent of the grapes are made into wine; the rest are eaten. Despite strenuous efforts from some of Turkey's leaders to induce the populace to drink wine, the Moslems of that country remain firm in their abstention.

Three-quarters of the wine in the world comes from Europe, specifically the countries bordering the Mediterranean Sea. Wine originated in this area and has been consumed there for over two thousand years. The countries with the highest per capita consumption are France, Italy, Portugal, Argentina, and Spain. Although many countries now show a decline in wine consumption, the figures are rising in the United States and Russia, and other countries of the former communist bloc.

None of this activity affects the serene vineyards that produce the truly great wines of the world. Most of them are in small, difficult areas, where the right combination of soil, sun, temperature, and humidity combine with the skill of the vintner to create memorable wines. Some of the greatest wines come from tiny vineyards, some only a few acres in size. The commercial wine industry concerns itself mainly with making ordinary wine, easy to produce and profitable to sell.

It was the ancient Greeks who first ennobled wine, praising it in song and story, and giving us unforgettable pictures on vases and wine cups. Although no one can say for certain what Greek wine tasted like, it is a fair assumption that by today's standards it would be considered inferior. The Greeks watered down their wine and added resin for taste (or to mask the taste), an indication that something may have been lacking.

The Romans recognized the importance of wine to the economy, and encouraged the citizenry to drink in order to increase tax revenues. The first historically great wine was Opimian, first produced around 121 B.C. Roman wines were made in barrels and were bottled before serving, unlike the Greek wines, which were made in clay amphoras. When the Romans invaded Gaul (modern France) they planted vineyards. By the fifth century A.D. the Romans had left behind a network of vineyards that eventually became the beginning of the great French wine industry.

When Christianity became dominant in the Dark Ages following the end of the Roman empire, wine became associated with the church. It was considered symbolic of the blood of Christ, part of the ritual, and one of the good things in life. Vineyards sprouted in the shadow of great monasteries, tended by diligent monks who slowly refined the process of wine-making over the centuries, developing regional wines and techniques of fermenting still in use today.

Until the 17th century wine was aged and stored in barrels. When one barrel spoiled, the entire contents was lost. Some unknown monk discovered that if wine was bottled and plugged with a new invention, the cork, it lasted longer and improved with age in the bottle.

Seventeenth century Englishmen developed a taste for the delicate wine of Champagne, France. When they received barrels from Champagne, they immediately removed the wine and bottled it. They quickly discovered that the fermentation process not only continued in the bottle (the second fermentation), but produced an effervescent wine far superior to that which arrived earlier in barrels. Although the matter is often disputed, it may be that the English should be credited for discovering modern champagne.

It was a Frenchman, however, who perfected the bubbly when he invented the cork tied with string, the stronger bottle that would not burst, and the practice of blending different wines to create a superior flavor. His name was Dom Perignon, cellar-master in the Abbey of Hautvilliers in the latter part of the 17th century.

Early bottles were often shaped like decanters to make serving easier, and to help them stand upright. This, however, allowed the cork to dry out and ruin the wine. From 1700 to 1800 bottles evolved into their present shape when it was discovered that bottles stored on their sides permitted the cork to stay wet and supple, keeping out air and thus preserving the wine.

Great wine depends on a combination of factors for its greatness, such as climate, type of grape, and how it is grown and made. The high prices of many fine wines are not arrived at arbitrarily, but are based on the economics of producing something of quality. The vines that produce great wine must be pruned; the greater the wine, the more the pruning. This limits the amount of grapes each vine can produce, making the end product scarcer than ordinary wines whose vines require less pruning.

Great wine is aged in brand-new, unseasoned oak barrels. Much of the wine evaporates through the barrel. Lesser quality wine can subsequently be matured in the used barrels. Ordinary wine is matured in vats.

The expense of new barrels, the small supply of superior grapes, and the labor-intensiveness of producing great wine, all add to the cost. Mass tastes favor lesser-quality wines at lower prices. The market for great wines is small, as is their production. If the mass market ever demanded great wine and was willing and able to pay the price, there would be no shortage of it. Supply and demand and the rigid rules of economics determine, in the end, how much great wine will be produced each year.

Wine can be made from anything juicy that contains sugar and has a pleasant taste. Ceremonial wines are often made from berries and fruits such as blackberries, elderberries, and cherries. Dandelions make an interesting wine, and in Japan, sake, wine made from rice, is a major industry. While it is possible to make wine from almost any fruit or vegetable that contains sugar, the finished product must have a light, pleasant, and refreshing taste, and possess that indefinable quality called character. It is a subjective quality and is the reason wine-tasters exist. There will probably never be much of a market for beet or yam wine, even if some enterprising vintner decided to take the risk.

Of the many varieties of grapes, only fifty are made into wine, and of these, only around twenty-five can be considered important. Some wines bear the name of the grape they are made with, such as cabernet sauvignon; others are hardly known outside of the industry, such as tintas, used to make port wine, and the palomino grape, used for sherry.

Some of the important grapes used to make wine are cabernet sauvignon (Bordeaux reds), carignan (red table-wine from France), catawba (native American sparkling wine), chardonnay (white burgundy, Chablis, Montrachet, Meursault, Pouilly-Fuisse, champagne), chenin blanc (Vouvray, Coteaux du Layon, Savennieres), folle blanche (Cognac, and other wines), gamay (Beaujolais, rosé), grenache (Châteauneuf-du-Pape, Tavel, various rosés), kerner (a new German grape), merlot, Muller-Thurgau, muscat (muscatel—the muscat is one of the historic grapes used to make wine by the ancient Greeks), pinot blanc, pinot noir (a fine quality red wine grape, often used for champagne), palomino (sherry), riesling, sangiovese (Chianti), sauvignon blanc (Bordeaux, Graves, sauternes), semillon (sauternes), seyval blanc (French/American hybrid), sylvaner, syrah (Hermitage, Shiraz; may be called petite syrah in California), traminer, welschriesling (the name means "foreign reisling," and it is used to make reisling type wines in various countries), zinfandel (grows primarily in California).

Although the process of wine-making is complex, and the thousands of years of accumulated tradition seems forbidding to the novice, making wine is deceptively simple. Each grape is a winery all by itself. Thirty percent of the pulp of a grape is sugar. Natural yeast from the atmosphere coats the skin of every grape. When the grape is crushed, the yeast comes in contact with the sugar inside the grape and begins fermenting it, turning it into alcohol. Crush a grape in your fingers and you have set into motion a tiny winery and, under the right conditions, you will soon have real wine.

Of course, this is like saying that a ballet consists of people on a stage jumping around in time to some music; basically true, but hardly a description of a complex art. So it is with wine. Amateur wine-makers, like amateur beer-brewers, can make wine in their homes, some of it very good, indeed. But to make anything higher in quality than good wine takes money, hard work, the dedication of a monk, endless amounts of time, and some luck.

It has been said that making great wine is an art. If that is true, a bottle of great wine has two important advantages for the art lover: it is the only art which can be consumed, and it is the only art still within the price range of the average person.

How Do You Say Drunk *in Latin?*

The emperor Claudius had a reputation for getting drunk at every meal and Nero (A.D. 54 to 68), who succeeded him after his mother, Aggripina, poisoned Claudius and named Nero emperor, loved the grape so well that he introduced 159 holidays that required heavy drinking. Claudius and Nero made wine available free at the taxpayer's expense, to encourage drinking.

The Romans had eleven words for drunkenness. After a few sips of wine, one could become *ebriolus,* slightly tipsy. *Madescere* meant to get drunk, and when Bacchus finally took over, one became *ebriulatus,* tipsy. To be intoxicated one was said to be *ebriacus,* or *uvidus,* in one's cups. When a Roman was full of wine, he was *vinolentus.* He proceeded from there to *vino madens,* being fully drunk, and finally to *vino mersus,* dead drunk. Someone four sheets to the wind was *ebrius* in old Rome. A riotous drunk was *temulentus,* and if a citizen could not pronounce *intemperantissimae perpotationes,* he was obviously swizzled.

What the Romans imbibed to become comatose was *ebriamen,* an intoxicating drink, and if he made a habit of it, he was *ebriositas,* an alcoholic. When he slept it off and awoke, he was *sobrius.*

Inebriation, said a wit, is when you feel sophisticated but can't pronounce it. Before we laugh at the drunken Romans, see how many words mean the same thing in English: inebriated, looped, drunken, bombed, intoxicated, crocked, high, juiced, sloshed, besotted, loaded, pixilated, plastered, polluted, smashed, stoned, tight, tanked, pickled, soused, pie-eyed, cockeyed, blitzed, hammered, wasted, paralyzed, swizzled, tipsy. That's seventeen more than the Romans had.

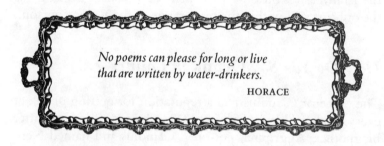

*No poems can please for long or live
that are written by water-drinkers.*

HORACE

A Food Lover's Abecedary

A search through the vocabulary of food yields interesting and sometimes amusing results. (*Satire* for example, originally meant "fruit salad." (The root word of *fruit* means "enjoy.") Discoveries are endless. Food words have worked themselves into the daily language of every culture; metaphors echo in every tongue. Modern cockney rhyming slang for money is "milk-and-honey." Cornucopia was the original horn of plenty, which, when taken off the goat that suckled Zeus, yielded fruit without end. Slot machines spin daily, and it is pictures of fruit that create the winner's jackpot and the loser's fruit salad. If you want to describe the meaning of life, you can do no better than to start with food words.

ABSINTHE may make the heart grow fonder, but it destroys the brain with its main ingredient, wormwood. Absinthe was banned in France in 1915. In anticipation of the presumed needs of absinthe addicts, the development of Pernod was underwritten by the French government to take the place of absinthe when it was removed from the marketplace. Wormwood was originally thought to cure intestinal worms; at least it was an excuse to drink the stuff. Vermouth, at one time, also contained wormwood.

ALCOHOL was named after *Al-kohl,* a paste made from antimony and used as a cosmetic by Egyptian women in the days of the Pharaohs. The Arabic word came to mean anything that was a fine extract of something.

APPLE comes from the province of Italy called Abela, where the modern apple is thought to have first appeared. The phrase "apple pie order" used to indicate neatness, has nothing to do with apples. According to one source, it comes from the French phrase *nappe plie'e en ordre* and means: "the linen folded in order," instructions to a French maid to fold the linens. It sounded like "apple-pie order," to the unlearned of America and the phrase stuck.

APRICOT comes from the Latin *praecos* which means "early ripening," a reference to the fruit's appearance early in the season. Precocious comes from the same root. The first reference to this early ripening member of the rose family, midway between a peach and a plum, was in 1578.

ARTICHOKES look a little like thistles. Even their color is light green, almost blue, as are thistles. The Arabs called it *al kharsuf,* "a thistle." The Italians changed it into *articiocco,* and the English into *artichoke.*

BACON comes from the Middle High German word *backe,* meaning the rear part, "the back." In old England it changed to *bacoun.* A *rasher* (one slice of bacon), comes from *rash,* meaning to cut. The words *razor* and *raze* have the same root. In twelfth-century England a side of bacon was given to any man who could enter the church in Dunmow and swear upon the Bible that he had not fought with his wife for twelve months and one day. The worthy citizen who would make such a vow would "bring home the bacon."

BAKER'S DOZEN. The practice of giving a customer thirteen items when twelve were ordered originated in England where penalties were levied for short-weighting a customer. Baker's scales were often not accurate so the baker gave an extra loaf or roll to make sure he didn't break the law, and to also encourage the customer to continue patronizing his shop. In Egypt, bakers caught short-weighting their customers were nailed to the door of their shop by their ears.

BANANA is a Portuguese word for a fruit known throughout history. The original food for thought, its botanical name is *musa sapientum,* "the man who thinks," said to come from the legend of wise men who sat under the shade of the tree, eating bananas. The banana is an herb, not a tree.

BARBECUE comes from the Haitian word *barbacoa* meaning "a frame to roast meat on." George Washington mentions barbecues in his journal and Alexander Pope refers to them as well.

BEETS reminded early cooks of a bleeding animal when they cut them open, so they called them beets, from the French word *bête,* meaning "beast."

BING CHERRY was named after Ah Bing, a Chinese gardener in the United States. Although Ah Bing gave us this great gift, he died in poverty. (*See also* cherry.)

BOBORYGMOLOGY. The study of stomach rumblings.

BRANDY is derived from the Dutch *brandewijn,* meaning "wine that has been burned," a reference to wine distilled over fire.

BROCCOLI means "little sprout" in Italian. A broccoli is a cauliflower that doesn't form a head. The Romans called it *brocca,* "pointed stick."

BUTCHER in old France was called *bouchier,* one who killed goats. *Bouchiers* were forbidden to kill goats in public. If one of them violated this law the authorities could "get his goat."

BUTTER means "cow cheese." It is a combination of two Greek words, *bous,* meaning "cow," and *tyros,* meaning "cheese": thus *boutyros.*

CAESAR SALAD is not a dish of ancient Rome but was invented in 1927 by Alex Cardini in Tijuana, Mexico, just across the border from San Diego. His brother Caesar owned a restaurant there. Alex originally called it an "Aviator's Salad," but apparently the bonds of fraternal devotion (or employment) inspired a change of name. Caesar's Hotel in Tijuana still serves it to tourists, who are not quite sure they can believe the story.

CANDY comes from the Sanskrit word *khanda,* meaning "a piece of sugar" or "a small bit." It is both a noun and a verb, describing the process of crystallizing sugar or molasses as well as the finished product. Fruit or flower petals cooked in sugar and allowed to crystallize with it are *candied,* and become *candy.* Later definitions were expanded to cover other treats made with different ingredients and processes, which the British lump together under the title *sweets,* or *sweetmeats,* and others call *confections.* The first true confectioner was an ancient Egyptian.

CANTALOUPE comes from India, but was named by the Italians after the village of Cantalupo. The Pope had a country home in that town and it was there that the melon was first grown successfully outside India.

CASHEW was originally an East Indian word, *acajou,* named from the *acaiaba* tree on which the nut grows.

CHEESE. When the ancient Greeks drained the whey from the curds in the process of making cheese they used a wicker basket called a *formos.* The Romans called it *forma,* and the modern Italians, *formaggio,* which no longer describes the basket, but the cheese itself. The French call cheese *fromage.* The original

Greek and Latin words entered the English language as the important and useful word, *form*, referring to anything which gives shape to something, or the shape itself.

The Latin word for cheese is *caseus*, and the Urdu word is *chiz*, from which the modern English word is derived, as well as the Spanish word for cheese, *queso*. In the Medieval cheese markets of Holland and other countries, only the wealthy could afford the largest wheels of cheese. Anyone with enough money to purchase the biggest wheels were important people, and were called *big wheels*, or *big cheeses*.

CHERRY was named by the Romans after a city called *Cerasus*, presumably where the fruit originated. *Cerise*, a red the color of cherries, comes from the same source.

CHIVES is derived from *caepa*, the Latin word for onions. It became *cive* in French.

CHOWDER comes from the practice of French fishermen on the coast of Brittany of throwing some of their daily catch into a community pot, a *chaudière*, so all could eat.

CLOVE. The Romans thought this pungent spice resembled nails, and named it *clovis*, "nails."

COBB SALAD, a refreshing mixture of shredded vegetables, was invented by Robert H. "King" Cobb, of The Brown Derby restaurant in Beverly Hills, California. Cobb also invented a harmless concoction of soda water and flavored syrups that allowed children the fantasy of drinking a real cocktail with their parents. He named it the "Shirley Temple," in honor of the most famous child star of the times.

COCONUT comes from the Spanish *coco*, meaning a grimacing face, and named for the three dark spots on the bottom of a coconut that resemble a human, or monkey, face.

THE SECRET LIFE OF FOOD

COLE SLAW is a combination of two Dutch words: *koolsa* from cabbage and *sla,* from salad.

CONDIMENT. Roman women preserved and pickled food by adding spices to brine or vinegar. The name for the process in Latin was *condimentum.* Today only the spices are called condiments.

CORN comes from the Old Norse word *korn,* which means a grain-sized lump of something.

CREAM. The original Greek root was *chrisma,* meaning an unguent. *Christ* is also a Greek word from the same root, and means "the anointed." *Chrisma* changed into *cresme* in Old French and *crayme* in Middle English, and finally ended as *cream,* the top of the milk, or the best (top) of anything: "the cream of the crop."

DESSERT comes from the French word *desservir,* which means "to remove all the dishes from the table" (to make room for the final course, the fruit or cake served to sweeten the palate).

DINNER is from the French word *dîner,* to dine. It is derived, in turn, from the Latin words *dis* (away), and *jejunare* (to fast). It means "to break a fast," and so refers to either breakfast or dinner. In French, dinner is *déjeuner,* and breakfast is *petit déjeuner,* (a small dinner).

FILBERT. This delicious nut ripens on St. Philibert's Day, August 22, and so bears the name of the Burgundian saint.

FRUIT. The original meaning of this word was "enjoy," from the Latin *fructus.* As late as the eighteenth century, vegetables were referred to as fruits.

FOOD and FODDER both come to us from the Old English word *foda* meaning "that which sustains, or keeps active."

FOWL is from the Teutonic word *fleugan,* which means "to fly." The Anglo-Saxons called meat that flies *fugol;* in Middle English it changed to *foul,* or *fowel.*

GARLIC comes from Old English and means *spear leek.* During the Middle Ages bald men were called *pilgarlics* (peeled garlics).

GRAPE. This Latin word entered the language during the eleventh century at the time of the Norman conquests. A grape was the hook used to wrest the fruit from the vine. Eventually, the fruit itself was named after the harvesting tool. When the farmer had difficulty with the vine he had to *grapple* with the tool.

HALIBUT is a certain kind of fish called *butt-fish,* which was only eaten during holy days in medieval England, the "holy-butt."

HASH. Surprise! The French invented hash, or at least the word for it. This truck-stop staple has its origins in *hache,* meaning "to chop."

HORS D'OEUVRES means "outside the works," or, something to eat that is not part of the dinner. *Oeuvres,* "the works," is derived from *oeuf,* the French word for egg. The term has been borrowed by the art world and means "the entire life work of one artist."

HUMBLE PIE is derived from a dish of the same name made of unwanted organs and other animal parts left after the cooks took the best cuts for the meat pies served to the upper classes. Humble pie was the pie of peasants. The word, in use since 1642, comes from the Latin *lumbus,* meaning "loin." Someone who has been chastised is said to have eaten humble pie.

JERUSALEM ARTICHOKE is not an artichoke and has nothing to do with Jerusalem. It is a tuber, like the potato, which grows on the roots of the American sunflower. The flavor reminds some of artichokes. Jerusalem is a substitute word for *girasole,* Italian for sunflower. When first introduced, the word *girasole* was difficult for Americans to remember, so a more familiar word which sounded like it was substituted. A more accurate name, *sun chokes* is being fielded as a substitute but has not caught on terribly well.

KETCHUP (the accepted spelling; or catsup) was originally a Chinese word, *katsup,* that meant "pickled fish sauce." The Malaysians transformed it to kechup. In the United States we dropped fish from the recipe, added tomatoes, and put the letter *t* into the word.

KITCHEN came from the Latin word *coquina* (changed to *cycene* in Old English), and signified the room in which the cook (*co-quere*) prepared meals. The part of the castle containing the treasure of the lord was the keep. The soldier in charge was the keeper. The word was also used to signify the part of a house in which food was stored and prepared. The person in charge of food storage was the house-keeper. Eighteenth-century American kitchens were called *keeping-rooms.*

KIWI is a thin-skinned berry with a succulent jade interior, and is named after a New Zealand bird. Add a beak and bird legs and the hairy brown exterior could pass for a bird in a dim light. The kiwi is really from China, where it was called *yang tao.* It was re-christened the Chinese gooseberry when vines were imported to New Zealand in 1906. It is neither a gooseberry nor of the same family. A curiosity in the United States, they rotted by the tons in store bins when they were first imported in 1953, until some inspired grocer renamed it the kiwi. The rest is marketing history, and the born-again kiwi appears everywhere today, a reliable ingredient in pastries and desserts.

LEEK comes from the Old English word *leac* meaning "spear."

LOBSTER NEWBURG should be called Lobster Wenberg. A customer and friend of the owner of Delmonico's restaurant in New York City invented the specialty and it became an instant hit. Delmonico intended to name the dish Lobster Wenberg after its inventor, but the two men had a falling-out. The angry Delmonico spitefully named the dish Lobster Newburg after a town in New York state called Newburgh. (No one can explain what additional spite drove him to drop the final *h*.)

MACADAMIA NUT should have been called the von Mueller nut, after Ferdinand von Mueller, who discovered it in the 1850s. He named it after his friend, Dr. John Macadam, a Scotsman who practiced medicine in Australia. The man for whom this famous nut was named never tasted it. Dr. Macadam died of pleurisy aboard the ship taking him to New Zealand where he intended to sample the nut which bore his name.

MACARONI comes from the Middle Italian word *maccare,* meaning to pound something, a reference to the making of dough. The word *macaroon* comes from the same root. During the American Revolution the English sang a derisive song about the Yankee who "stuck a feather in his hat and called it macaroni." The reference was to the Maccaroni club in England during the period of the Revolution, whose members were fops, gamblers, and show-offs—objects of derision. The Yankees loved the song and adopted it as their own, deflating British propaganda and launching an American folk song.

MARGARINE was originally made from hog fat, which resembled the color and sheen of pearls. In Spanish, *margarita,* and in French, *marguerite,* mean pearl.

MARMALADE. When Mary, Queen of Scots was out of sorts, which happened regularly in her hectic life, the only thing that would cheer her up was orange conserve. "Mary's illness" in French is "*Marie malade,* shortened to *marmalade.* Some etymologists claim the word really comes from the Latin *melimelum,* "sweet apple," but perhaps they are a bit too conservative.

MELBA TOAST, a dry, thin toast served with tea and jam, and PEACH MELBA, a dessert made with peach halves, ice cream, and a sauce of raisins and raspberries, were both named after Nellie Melba, the *toast* of three continents and one of the most famous opera singers in the world at the turn of the twentieth century. She took her stage name from Melbourne, Australia, where she was born.

MILK is an Anglo-Saxon word from the original *meoluc,* meaning, "to stroke," referring to the act of milking a cow or goat.

MUTTON, in the Late Latin *multo,* was a gold coin with a picture of a sheep on it. By the time Middle English got the word, the coin was called *motoun.* The connection with coins disappeared in the nineteenth century, although Sir Walter Scott mentioned it in a poem, *The Fair Maid of Perth,* in 1828.

NUT comes from the Old English *hnutu* and the Latin *nux,* or *nutriens,* meaning "to nourish."

ONION is a doublet of the word *union*—meaning both words are similar but entered the language through different routes. The word was created by adding the onion-shaped letter *o* to the word *union,* yielding the new spelling *ounion.* The letter *u* was later dropped to create the modern spelling. A union is something that is indivisible and which, if taken apart, is destroyed in the process, like an onion. The original root of the word is the Latin *un,* meaning "the number one," the only number that is not further divisible.

ORANGE. When oranges came to us from Persia (*naranj*) via Spain *naranja* they presented English-speaking people with the problem of pronouncing *an naranja,* an awkward combination. *Noncing,* the practice of adding or subtracting the letter *n,* saved

the day. The fruit became known as *an aranj,* and evolved to *an orange.* Some etymologists believe the first two letters are from the French *or,* meaning "gold," and refer to the golden color of the fruit.

OYSTERS got their name from the Greek *ostrakon,* meaning "hard shelled." The Romans called it *ostrea,* the first two letters *os* meaning bone. The oyster shell reminded the Romans of bones.

PAPRIKA has almost become synonymous with Hungary, the country that raised the spice to the highest culinary levels. It started out, like so many other words, in Greece, where it was called *peperi,* another word for pepper.

PÂTÉ is a fancy French way of saying *paste,* an Old French word that the Italians changed to *pasta.* The root word is the Greek *passein,* meaning the sprinkling of salt over a mess of food, or *patties,* another word derived from the same source.

PEA is derived from the Latin *pisum,* and came into English as *pease.* In the early 1700s the last two letters were dropped, giving us the modern spelling.

PEACH. The peach originated in China and the Latin name given it was *Malum persicum,* which really means "Persian apple." To the Europeans who named it, Persia was as remote as China. The name evolved into *peach* over the centuries.

PECAN is an American Indian word. The Algonquins called any nut *pakan,* in their Cree language.

PIE is a Middle English word, short for *magpie,* a reference to the nest of this thieving bird, filled with all sorts of different scavenged material. Early pies were filled with fruits, vegetables, or whatever meat was at hand, and reminded the cooks of a magpie nest.

POACHED EGG means "egg-in-a-bag," or *poche,* from the French word. When an egg is poached, the white of the egg forms a pocket around the yolk; hence the name.

POMEGRANATE, formerly called a Chinese Apple, is a combination of two words. The Spanish call them *granates,* derived from the root *grain;* a bulbous mass of seeds. The Moors brought them to Spain and the grateful Spanish named an entire city, *Granada,* after them. The streets in Granada were once lined with pomegranate trees. Semi-precious stones were named after them: garnets. This fruit, with its seeds of crimson liquid capsules that burst forth, also gave its name to the grenade. The pomegranate was sacred to Demeter, goddess of agriculture, and the French, who name everything that looks like an apple a *pomme,* called them *pomme de grenate.*

RADISH comes from the Latin root *radix,* meaning root. When something is eradicated, it is pulled out by the root.

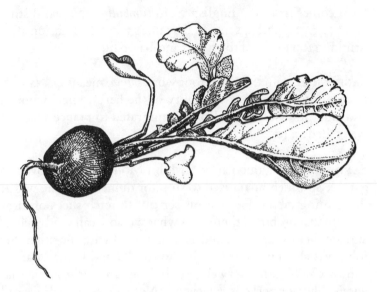

RELISH comes to us from *relaissier,* an archaic French word meaning "to leave something behind." It refers to the taste left in the mouth after eating a sauce of chopped pickles. When you think of something you did, or ate, that was pleasant, you *relish* the thought. Today, the sauce itself is called relish.

RHUBARB is named after the Volga River in Russia. The Greeks called it *rhabarbaron. Rha* means "Volga River," and *barbaron* means "foreign," or "barbaric," because the first rhubarbs were imported from Russia.

ROSEMARY is an herb with a truly poetic name. It comes from the Latin *ros,* "dew," and *marinus,* "ocean," or "marine"; in other words, like a sea-breeze, moist and fragrant. Sometime during the Middle Ages the word *rosmarinus* was changed to *rosemary* in honor of the mother of Jesus, whose name was linked to the flower.

RUM comes from the English word *rumbullion,* a great disturbance, a riot—perhaps inspired by one's mental condition after drinking too much of the sugarcane-based liquor.

SAGE comes from the Latin root word *salvia,* meaning "safe," a reference to the purported ability of the herb to heal wounds and cure illnesses. From Rome it migrated to France where it was called *sauge.*

SANDWICH was named after Sir John Montagu, who loved to gamble so much he refused to stop for dinner when he was at the gaming tables. He sent his servant to fetch slices of meat and bread, combined them into what we now call sandwiches, and ate them with one hand as he gambled with the other. Sir John was also First Lord of the Admiralty and Fourth Earl of Sandwich. We came very close to having sandwiches called *admirals, johns,* or perhaps *montagues.* (Not so far-fetched; we call certain sandwiches *submarines* today.) On the other hand, if Sir John had not loved gambling better than sailing, we may never have had a sandwich at all and might still be subjects of the Crown; the American Revolution was taking place at the time.

SAUCE. One of many words derived from *sal,* the Latin word for salt. There are dozens more, such as salami, salivate, salary, salsa, salad, sausage, saucer, saucy, salute. Salt is the cornerstone of cooking and the most important seasoning we use.

SCALLIONS were onions grown in Biblical Ashkelon, where they were called *ascalons.* Today the term is used to mean new or spring onions, the entire onion plant before the bulb swells.

SCROD is a young cod fish that is split in order to cook it. From the Middle Dutch *schrode,* meaning something split, or cut away.

SEASONING was originally a way of saying "ripening." From the French *saison,* it refers to the season of the year in which fruit, if left to itself, will ripen automatically and taste better than fruit picked unripe and left to ripen in the pantry. Later on, something added to food to make it taste better was called *seasoning,* and the original reference to tree- or vine-ripening was lost.

SHRIMP comes from the German word *schrumpfen,* meaning something that has shriveled, or gotten smaller—as some store-bought shrimp seem to do when cooked.

SIRLOIN. This choice cut of steak was *not* named by Henry VIII, or any of several other English monarchs alleged to have knighted it *Sir Loin* after a particularly fine repast. It's a great story but untrue. The word comes from a less interesting ancestor, the French word *surlonge,* which means "over the loin."

SOLE comes from the Latin root *solum,* meaning "the ground" or "earth" (soil). The Romans called the fish *solea,* and applied the same word to the bottom of the foot, which came in contact with the earth and resembled the flat fish (or so thought the Romans).

SPAGHETTI comes from the Italian *spago,* meaning "strings."

SPICE derives from the Latin word *species,* meaning "something of a kind" or "to sort things out" into recognizable types. In the Middle Ages, saffron, cloves, cinnamon, and nutmeg were the four *species* sold by grocers to preserve food and sometimes as medicine.

SQUASH sounds like what you do to it after you bake it. The word was a compromise by the early settlers who encountered what the Algonquin Indians called *isquonterquashes* in 1634.

The Indian word means "something you eat raw." The Pilgrims preferred to cook it, and shortened its name.

STEAK. We owe the name of our most popular cut of meat to Iceland. The Icelanders called the spit on which they roasted their meat a *steikja,* meaning "a stick of wood." The word goes back past the 1500s, into the mists of Viking feasts.

TANGERINE is named for Tangiers, a port in Morocco. The tangerine was once referred to as "the kid-glove orange" because its skin slipped off as easily as a glove and had the feel of fine leather.

TARRAGON began menacingly as the Greek word *drakon,* "dragon." It became *targone* in Italian and *estragon* in French.

TODDY, a traditional hot drink made of whiskey, hot water, lemon and cloves, was originally a drink from India, made from fermented palm sap. It was called *tadi* in Hindustani.

TOMATO was derived from the Aztec word *tomatl.*

TORTONI was invented by an Italian *glacier,* or ice-cream maker, in Paris around 1810. Tortoni was the manager of the Pavillon du Hanovre, a pleasure palace where people gathered to dine, enjoy sweet desserts and coffees, wander through the display gardens, listen to concerts and dance at the balls, and watch the fireworks every night. The entrepreneur with the latest concoction would draw the biggest crowds. When Tortoni invented his frozen cream *mousse,* packed with almonds and macaroons and flavored generously with rum, it was a sensation and quickly became a classic dessert.

TURNIP means "round turnip," from the French *tour* "to turn around," and the Latin *napus,* a turnip. European turnips are more popular than the little ones we see in the United States. In

Scotland the turnip is an important food, and grow so large they are often carved like pumpkins at Halloween.

VERMICELLI means "little worms" in Latin, a far too accurate description of a certain type of pasta.

VITAMIN was coined from the Latin *vita,* meaning "life," and *amino,* referring to the group of acids that form the basis of the protein molecule. The word was the source of a bitter fight between two researchers, Casimir Funk and Frederick Hopkins, both of whom claimed to have discovered vitamins. (Hopkins generally gets the credit.)

VEAL originally meant "year" in the Indo-European tongues. From the root *wetos* it evolved to mean a calf that was one year old. The connection to the calendar was lost by the time of the Roman empire when it was known as *vitellus,* from which root an archaic slang word for food, *vittles,* is possibly derived. *Victuals,* another word meaning food, comes from the Latin *victus,* from which springs the word *victor,* someone who has conquered obstacles. Such words are virtually impossible to trace accurately, but the connection between conquest and an assured food supply is a strong one.

VENISON comes from the Latin *venari,* "to hunt." When the word reached France as *venaison,* it meant the flesh of any edible wild animal. In England as *veneison* its meaning was narrowed to mean only the meat of wild deer.

VINEGAR is simply a description of a versatile liquid. It means "sour," or "rough wine"; *vin agre* in Old French.

WALNUT is a combination of two Anglo-Saxon words: *wealh,* "foreigners," and *hnutu,* "nut." Because walnuts were imported into England they were dubbed *wealhhnutu,* "the foreign nut."

WHEAT is the second most important food in the world (rice is number one) in terms of how many people depend on it as the basis for their diet. We owe the early Germans for its name, *hweit,* meaning "white."

YAM comes from the Senegalese word *nyami,* "eat."

ZEST. Let's end our journey through the etymology of food with a word that began in the kitchen and worked its way into general use. Zest is a French word and means the thin, outer peel of a citrus fruit from which the white, pulpy underskin has been scraped away. The oil-filled surface skin is then minced and added to a variety of main courses and desserts to impart a lively, piquant flavor. Zest still retains its original meaning but has also come to mean a lively, keen enjoyment, an agreeable excitement. No one knows where the word came from, but it perfectly describes the right attitude towards all manner of food.

Chapter 3

Where Foods Come From

*There is no love sincerer
than the love of food.*

George Bernard Shaw

The Rebirth of French Wine

The French wine industry owes a debt of gratitude to the good vintners of Chile, that long, narrow country that seals Argentina's west coast from the Pacific Ocean like a gold inlay. Chile produces some of the finest and most underrated wines in the world. It's no wonder, because the vines of Chile were carefully culled from the vineyards of France and Germany and imported by the dons sent to colonize New Spain over three hundred years ago so that they would have a supply of fine wine to ease the rigors of colonialism. Alone among the vineyards of the world, Chilean grapes grow on their own roots. The rest of the world's wine grapes are grafted onto different root stock.

In the early 1860s the North American vine louse *Phylloxera vitifoliae* wiped out vineyards all over Europe. The French vineyards were hit hardest: 2.5 million acres were destroyed; madeira disappeared completely, and the survival of the industry was in jeopardy.

The vineyards of Chile were protected on the west by the Pacific Ocean, on the east by the towering Andes mountains, a

69

natural boundary between Chile and Argentina, and on the north by the sand dunes of the Atacama desert.

The Chileans sent cuttings of their vineyards, descendants of the original French vines, back to France to repopulate the decimated vineyards. Other areas untouched by the vine-louse, such as California, also sent cuttings.

The great international fraternity of vintners—like the vines they grow—are intertwined and depend upon each other for support in difficult times.

The Oldest Beer in the World

And thou shalt give to me to eat until I am satisfied,
And thou shalt give to me beer until I am drunk,
And thou shalt establish my issue as kings,
forever and ever.

> Prayer to Osiris (God of The Dead)
> Ramses IV (Circa 1200 B.C.)

To Julius Caesar, beer was "the high and mighty liquor," a comforting and nourishing brew present from the beginning of civilization. Beer, made from fermented barley or the roots of plants such as sassafras, ginger, or spruce, was an important food of early civilizations. If crops were bad or the hunters returned empty-handed the tribe could always depend on beer, rich in nutrients, to ensure survival (and to take the edge off the disappointment). The pleasure induced by beer was further proof, if proof was needed, that the gods wanted people to drink beer.

Brewing beer was the province of women until the Industrial Revolution gave rise to giant breweries. *The Epic of Gilgamesh,* perhaps the oldest narrative in the world, written four thousand years before Christ, tells of a woman *brewster* (the feminine form of *brewer*) named Siduri who gave comfort, advice, and beer to Gilgamesh, the greatest of the Sumerian kings.

As you wash down a fiery dish of chili with a glass of suds, consider the Sumerian *sabtiem,* brewsters who added black pepper, powdered crab claws, hot spices, and tree bark to the brew. Beer was food to them, liquid bread, a meal in itself.

The broth brewed by the *sabtiem* was shared in a communal fashion, each drinker sitting around the pot, elbow-to-elbow with the others. This also led them to invent the drinking straw. As they gathered around the large, narrow-necked, clay beer jars, they poked long, hollow straws through the debris on the surface to get at the clear liquid beneath. (The privileged classes sported straws of gold or silver.) Such daily meetings bonded the drinkers as more than friends. Around the *broth* they were *brothers.* They would often drink this broth-from-the-gods in a *broth*-el (*el* is a Hebrew word meaning "God").

When the Vikings were thoroughly besotted they went *beer-serk.* In their bear-skin shirts (*berserkrs*) they terrorized the countryside like fearsome, two-legged bear-monsters with huge, menacing horns on their helmets. The word *beer* is related to *bear* and *berserk,* a description of the state induced by too much *aul,* Norse for beer, now called *ale.* Viking women drank as much *aul* as the men. In an alcoholic trance called *Bragg,* they could foretell the future. *Bragging* was an important part of Viking culture. Beer, they believed, came originally from the udders of a goat named *Heidrun* in Valhalla, a giant ale-house with 540 doors through which the dead entered to drink *aul,* eat roast pig, fight with their comrades, and swap tales of valor.

In the *Kalevala,* a Finnish creation myth, more words are devoted to the making of beer by women than to the creation of the earth itself. Although women were the brewsters of Europe they were not permitted to operate a tavern unless it was under their husband's name. Medieval ale-wives were held to strict account; punishment for not filling the flagons to the top was swift.

The Code of Hammurabi (1500–2000 B.C.) states, "If a beer seller does not receive barley as the price of beer, but if she receives money . . . or makes the beer measure smaller than the barley measure received, they shall throw her into the water."

Noted beer historian Alan Eames (who supplied much of the information in this section) claims that beer may have first been brewed at the end of the Pleistocene age, ten thousand years ago near the Amazon River, predating the Sumerians and Mesopotamians by thousands of years. If manioc cultivation was practiced by these early people, as Eames believes, then the Amazon was where beer first entered civilization. A real-life Indiana Jones who learned to read Egyptian hieroglyphics in his search for the beginnings of beer, Eames went up the Nile River and the Amazon and climbed the Andes, stein in hand, searching for ancient brewery sites.

Primitive beers were made by women who chewed grain until it became mushy with saliva. They spit the mash into vats; water was added and the mixture was heated. The vats were buried underground to allow the enzymes in the saliva to change the starches in the mash into sugar, which was then fermented by the yeast that dropped into the brew from exposure to air.

After two days it was dug up, ready to drink. Old engravings show South American Indians brewing beer in this manner. So important was beer to the Egyptians that tiny working models of breweries were buried with the dead so they could continue to enjoy beer in the next world. A three-thousand-year-old tomb yielded the following inscription: "Every man who worked for me was paid . . . they did it for beer and bread."

"When you can make a life-sustaining food that also makes you feel good, merely by using the brewing equipment in your mouth, you might conclude that a higher power put it there for that purpose," Eames suggests. "Almost every society on earth has made the connection between the making of beer and whatever god they believed in. In their view, it was a divine gift. By drinking the spirits in the bowl they fulfilled the wishes of the spirits they believed watched over their culture."

In the spirit of what one might call hands-on archaeology, Fritz Maytag, owner of San Francisco's Anchor Brewing Company, and Solomon Katz, an anthropologist at the University of Pennsylvania, brewed barley beer by a method they deduced from clues on clay tablets and carvings dating back 3,800 years. Using instructions from an ancient hymn, "You are the one who soaks the malt in a jar . . . the one who spreads the cooked mash on large reed mats," deductive reasoning (honey and dates must have been the sweet substance that was unnamed in the hymn), as well as their own intuition and experience, they made a beer from twice-baked loaves of barley bread (a way to store barley without spoilage) and other ingredients that they believed approximated the first beer.

They bottled 286 cases of the brew and named it Ninkasi Sumerian Beer. When Maytag introduced the beer during a brewer's convention, he offered a toast to the Sumerian goddess of beer, Ninkasi. "I was overwhelmed by the sense that we had summoned her," he said.

When Hiram Bingham discovered Machu Picchu he thought it may have been built to house the women charged with making *chicha,* the sacred Inca corn beer. *Chicha* is still made in South America, both as beer and as a non-alcoholic drink. It is available in powder form and cans (Inca Cola) at Latino markets in the United States.

The Aztecs also imbibed corn beer. Drunkenness was forbidden on pain of death to anyone under the age of fifty-two. A drunken Aztec was considered under the influence of a god. So important was drinking that the Aztecs had two gods of the hangover: Quatlapanqui, the "head-splitter," and Papaztac, the "nerveless." There were also gods of the fermenting vats, gods of the drunken ones, and gods whose function it was to lead drunks to death by drowning, and others to prevent them from dying. One day each year was the day of *Tepoxtecatl,* the god of drink. Anyone born on that day was doomed to be an alcoholic.

No additives in modern beer can match those of certain Amazon tribes who still make ceremonial brews containing ashes of their dead. The dwindling Lenca tribe of Central America uses sheep and goat droppings to fortify their daily brew. Recent discoveries of the journals of John Abrey, an early eighteenth-century English historian, indicate the presence of the bones of ancestors in certain English beers of the time.

Beer contains proteins and carbohydrates. A twelve-ounce serving provides 1.6 grams of protein, the same as 6.4 ounces of milk or a nine ounce portion of fish. Natural beers supply small amounts of B complex vitamins, potassium, calcium, sodium, phosphorus, magnesium, thiamine, niacin, riboflavin, pantothenic acid, pyridoxine, biotin, and the higher esters. They also contain traces of iron, manganese, copper, zinc, and chromium.

For a man who routinely risks his life in his single-minded pursuit of beer history, Eames' favorite quote concerns the absence of beer. It is from *The Song of The Harper,* and was found inscribed on the walls of the Chapel of King Inyotef of ancient Egypt:

> *"I kiss her,*
> *Her lips open,*
> *And I am drunk*
> *Without a beer."*

GO EASY ON THE BEER

From peasant to pharoah, the Egyptians loved their beer, and drank it every day. But even in the dawn of civilization, beer's dark side was recognized as a menace, as the hieroglyph illus-

Make not   thyself helpless   in drinking in the

beer shop   For will not   the words of thy report repeated

slip out from thy mouth without thy knowing that thou hast uttered them

Falling down   thy limbs   will be broken

no one will   give thee hand to help   as for thy

companions in the   swilling of beer   they will get up

and say   Away with the drunkard

trates. It comes from the reign of Ramses II, 19th Dynasty, 1350 B.C. and has been used by temperance groups in America in their tracts against drinking alcoholic beverages.

- The first beer brewed in England was made by the Picts, circa 250 B.C. It was made from heather and may have had hallucinogenic properties.
- Before the American Revolution, the Massachusetts legislature made beer the official "beverage of health." They were trying to eradicate demon rum and gin.
- Beer was first sold in bottles in 1850. Before that if you wanted some beer you had to go to a saloon or tavern and bring your own container, usually a small pail called a groaner, with a cover, handle, and spout.
- The Jivaro Indians of south Ecuador drink three to four gallons of mild beer per person, per day.

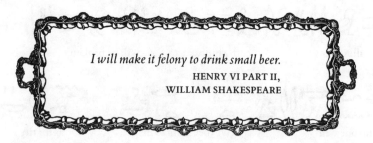

I will make it felony to drink small beer.
HENRY VI PART II,
WILLIAM SHAKESPEARE

The Greeks Had a Word for It: Cheesecake!

G. I. Joes pinned steamy photographs of actresses over their bunks in World War II and called them cheesecake; why they did so remains unrecorded (though, perhaps, not difficult to guess at). The ancient Greeks doted on cheesecake, typically baked in the shape of a woman's breast, thereby defining the connection between the libido and the taste buds, launching a pastry, and inventing a word—all three of which have survived almost two thousand years.

In *The Deipnosophists,* a fifteen-volume anthology compiled in A.D. 230 by the Greek scholar Athenaeus, an entire section was devoted to cheesecake, complete with recipes. Athenaeus tells us that the first cheesecake was baked on the island of Samos in the Aegean Sea. The cooks pounded cheese until it broke down into small pieces, then pressed it through a bronze sieve, added wheat flour and honey, and heated the mixture until it was done.

When it cooled, it made a cake so delicious that the people of Argos, a city-state, adopted the custom of having a wedding party for the friends of the groom, during which the bride-to-be served cheesecake to the guests. Gradually the practice evolved of serving the cake to all the guests at the wedding, and soon it became the highlight of the wedding feast. The traditional wedding cake comes from that beginning.

I Yam a Sweet Potato!

Let's hear it for the sweet potato, one of the most misunderstood vegetables. Often regarded as an inferior yam because it is paler and not as sweet as its African cousin, the sweet potato is a true potato and the real ancestor of the white potato.

Christopher Columbus, the first accidental tourist, didn't know where he was going, didn't know where he was when he got there, and didn't know what he was eating when the Arawaks, who he thought were Indians, served him sweet potatoes; he thought they were yams.

The Caribbean sweet potato Columbus brought to Queen Isabella quickly became popular and spread throughout Europe (mistakenly thought of, however, as a yam). The Arawak word for what they served Columbus was *batatas,* which evolved into the present word, *potatoes.* The white potato comes from the Andes, and did not make its appearance until later. When Falstaff said, "Let the sky rain potatoes," in William Shakespeare's play *The Merry Wives Of Windsor,* he was referring to sweet potatoes. In 1775, the Oxford English Dictionary legitimized the vegetable by first using the term *sweet potato*. After that, the white potato became simply the "potato," making our sweet hero seem to be a lesser form of white potato. Things have never been the same and the sweet potato's reputation has never recovered.

Sweet potatoes are more nutritious than yams, which are mostly sugar and starch. They contain vitamin A (carotene), vitamin C, calcium, iron, and pantothenic acid—helpful in metabolizing the carbohydrates of the potato—and traces of other important nutrients. Sweet potatoes do not keep as well as white potatoes (or yams), and tend to lose their delicate flavor if stored too long. They are not as profitable and there is a general consumer antipathy to them, as compared to our passionate love of white potatoes.

The sweet potato, confused with the yam and the white potato, has neither had the respect it deserves for its place in vegetable history nor the popularity its taste should have earned for it.

Pizza

Roman soldiers, accustomed to hearty loaves, tasted the flat matzoh of the Jews in Israel and found the unleavened bread lacked *focus,* the Latin word for hearth. They sprinkled herbs and crushed cheese on it, dribbled olive oil over the cheese, put it on a hot *focus,* and presto!, pizza pie was born. (In the Italian Bible, Elijah's manna is called *focaccia.*)

The origin of the word is found in the Latin *picea,* a description of the black coating caused by the burning fire found underneath a pizza crust. The Italian word *pizze* is roughly translated as "flat pie."

Roman bakers learned to make *focaccia* from the Greeks, masters of the art of baking, who in turn learned the trade from the Egyptians, who invented leavened bread. Pizza pie, basically a flat bread sprinkled with toppings and then baked, has been eaten around the Mediterranean in some form since the earliest days, but pizza as we know it today comes from pre-Renaissance Naples, Italy. Impoverished Neapolitan housewives had only the basic ingredients: olive oil, flour, lard, a bit of cheese, and herbs. Combining and baking these in ingenious ways, they slowly perfected their pies until all of Italy acclaimed them as the best.

After the suspicious Neapolitans convinced themselves that the yellow berries Columbus brought back from the New World were not poisonous, they began using tomatoes on their pizzas, creating the first *pizza al pomidoro* (with tomatoes). In the sixteenth century, pizza rose from the food of the teeming Neapolitan slums to the elevated tables of royalty. Maria Carolina, Queen of Naples, doted on the local pies and prevailed upon her husband, King Ferdinand IV, to permit their chef to make this peasant dish in the royal oven.

In 1889 Raffaele Esposito, a *pizzaiolo* (pizza chef) in Naples, had become so famous for his delicious pies that he was commanded by Queen Margherita to make pizza for a royal feast. The chef made three different kinds of pie for the occasion, one of which was designed to resemble the flag of Italy. Esposito used tomatoes for red, basil for green, and chose the whitest cheese he could find, mozzarella, for the white. The Queen was enchanted with the result. Although there are dozens of variations today, Pizza Margherita remains the basic pizza of America.

Neapolitan pizza is characterized by a thin crust and a light layer of toppings, baked to a crisp, golden brown. When the French adopted pizza, they used the basic recipe of Naples, but gave it a Gallic spin. The *pissaladieres* of France are redolent of the garlic and herbs of Provence. Although mozzarella is used, other French cheeses such as Gruyere, Roquefort, Port Salut, and Fontina are often added. Walnut oil is sometimes substituted for or added to olive oil, for the nutty flavor. *Pissaladiere* is usually baked in large trays and sold by weight.

Mezzaluna, "half-moon" pizza, also called *calzone,* is simply a folded-over pizza. A deep-fried *calzone* is called *pan-*

zerotti. Fancy pizzas, not usually seen in this country, include the *torta rustica,* a deep pizza stuffed with colorful ingredients and normally baked on holidays and special occasions.

The first pizzeria in the United States was opened in 1905 in New York City, at 53½ Spring Street, by Gennaro Lombardi. As pizzas became popular, *pizzaiolos* were accorded the same status that sushi chefs have today. Each *pizzaiolo* had a loyal and devoted following who claimed that his pies were the best available outside Italy.

American soldiers returned from World War II with an appetite for the new foods they ate abroad, and pizza was on the top of their list. By this time pizza parlors were not uncommon around the country. The stage was set for the next move: mass production.

As it does with everything it touches, the mass marketing of pizza resulted in the degradation of a once-noble dish. When all tomato sauce, cheese, and dough are made by machines in one central location, stored for weeks or months in refrigerated warehouses, shipped across the country on freight trains, and assembled for the consumer by technicians and not cooks, the result is the gooey, oleaginous mess that passes for pizza in much of the country today. It is a far cry from the real thing, made from the freshest of ingredients, baked until it is golden brown and crisp, and placed on your table hot and bubbly. Pizza has become, alas, fast food.

Although it is still a popular fast food, and will probably remain so, fine pizza has made a comeback with the advent of *nouvelle cuisine,* and its focus on the authentic dishes of other countries. Innovative chefs have brought pizzas to new levels of inventiveness, and pizza is now available on the menus of many gourmet restaurants, as well as traditional Italian restaurants, all over America.

The three main types of pizza served in the United States are the traditional Neapolitan pizza, sometimes called New York pizza, with a thin crust and a light arrangement of toppings, the deep-dish Chicago-style pie, and the California-

style pizza, a feather-light crust topped with rare delicacies, exotic cheeses, sun-dried tomatoes, and fancy mushrooms.

Pizza endures not only because it is delicious, but also because a few slices make an excellent balanced meal, containing starches (the flour crust), protein (cheese and other ingredients such as sausages, anchovies, etc.), and fresh vegetables (tomatoes and herbs). As the wise housewives of Naples knew long ago, a pizza pie is a logical solution to the need for inexpensive and satisfying nourishment, and one that children don't have to be urged to eat.

Granula, Granola, and Healthy Breakfast Foods

The health food movement in the United States was started by dedicated, strong people, many of whom conquered childhood weakness and disease through diet, exercise, and other methods considered radical by the medical establishment. They were often motivated by religious convictions and a messianic urge to bring their secrets to the world; a crusade against the godless and greedy who worshiped Mammon. Theirs was the path of righteousness, and it started with good health and self-discipline.

It was the age of the robber barons of American industry whose cavalier disregard for the welfare of the consuming public created a backlash army of crusading journalists that Theodore Roosevelt dubbed the Muckrakers, such as Upton Sinclair, Lincoln Steffens, and others who exposed the worst abuses of the exploiters.

Conditions were so abysmal in the food industry that only driven and dedicated people could overcome the obstacles posed by amoral businessmen, corrupt politicians, and a media only dimly aware of the frauds being perpetrated daily against an unsuspecting public.

Fortunately for the country, self-appointed guardians of the public health were sprouting like alfalfa seeds on an organic farm. Although they were regarded by the medical profession as radicals and crackpots, they continued to advocate healthful foods and to create innovative breakfast cereals and other nutritious products. Their actions and words helped to promote the importance of nutrition to the maintenance of good health and the eradication of nutrition-deficiency diseases like rickets, scurvy, and beri-beri.

One of the first was Dr. Caleb Jackson, a member of the Hygienist school of thought, who patented his cereal idea under the name *granula* in 1865. Dr. Jackson baked thin sheets of graham flour, broke them up, and baked the pieces a second time. The resulting cereal was so hard it had to be soaked overnight in milk and eaten the next morning. It was a financial flop but enjoyed a following among the Hygienists, who believed in exercise, proper nutrition, daily bathing, and other radical ideas of that era (including formidable breakfast foods).

GRANOLA AND CORN FLAKES

Although Jackson's *granula* lingered on, supported by followers of the Hygienist movement, two brothers, John and Will Kellogg, took the idea and ran with it. John, a medical doctor, invented a cereal similar to *granula*, but containing corn meal and oats. He marketed it under the same name and was promptly sued by Dr. Jackson. He changed the *u* to an *o* and *granola* was born. Dr. John Kellogg, a twenty-four-year-old workaholic, was already director of the Western Health Reform Institute's Battle Creek Sanatorium in Michigan, a mecca of nutritional thinking. A singularly strong-minded individual, he misspelled the name of his institution as *sanitarium,* and when corrected stood his ground, claiming his version of the word would become standard—which it did. Under his direction the sanitarium became the largest and most influential such institution in the country.

John and Will's parents had become Seventh-Day Adventists when their daughter died at the hands of incompetent doctors. They owned a broom corn farm (actually broom corn is a form of sorghum, and not true corn) in Connecticut at the time and little Will sold the brooms they made. The family moved to Battle Creek, Michigan, to be near the Adventists' sanitarium, which was under the direction of Elder White and Sister White, and opened a broom factory. A true visionary, Sister White was told in a vision to open a hospital and offer rest, vegetarian food, water therapy, and exercise to all who sought good health.

In 1894, John had his own vision. In a dream, he saw wheat being compressed into sheets. When he awoke, he and his brother started experimenting with the granola machinery, using wheat grains. Eventually they made a flake from wheat and began marketing it—to initial consumer resistance; people were used to eating hot cereal in the morning and the idea of a cold breakfast was not appealing.

Still, the Kelloggs were fascinated with the idea of cold breakfast cereals. Will Kellogg's idea was to develop one made of corn and he began tinkering. He developed flakes made of toasted corn meal and malt and dubbed them Kellogg's Corn Flakes, thereby launching the breakfast cereal industry and establishing a financial empire.

Fame and fortune, however, did not dim Dr. Kellogg's zeal for health. He continued to devote a good part of each day to writing about the virtues of clean, healthful living and pure food. Another of the comestibles invented by Dr. Kellogg for his patients was peanut butter, which quickly became popular. And the Kellogg brothers were not the only ones working on new foods. In Denver, Henry D. Perky was inventing Shredded Wheat.

At the age of forty-six, Will left the sanitarium and concentrated full-time on his cereals. Slowly, with massive and innovative advertising and promotion, the idea of cold cereals became acceptable. Finally, during the Depression, Kellogg's faith in his cereal became a reality when the American public accepted his ideas whole-heartedly and changed their eating habits permanently.

In 1891 C. W. Post was a patient of Dr. Kellogg's at the Battle Creek Sanitarium, and quickly absorbed the principles of the Hygienist movement. Like the Kellogg brothers, he was a Seventh-day Adventist with a keen business sense; too keen, some thought.

He founded a health spa of his own and a factory which churned out a stream of innovative products such as Grape Nuts, Postum (a substitute for coffee), and a boxed cereal that went head-to-head in the market place with Kellogg's Corn Flakes. He thunderingly proclaimed his competing cereal "Elijah's Mannah." The resulting uproar from the clergy was so overwhelming that he meekly renamed his cereal "Post Toasties."

The divines' intervention was a blessing in disguise. The re-christened cereal soon found its way into mass markets far beyond the health-food network of stores and spas and became a fixture in American households, making Post a millionaire. The popular appeal of the cereal was captured by a cartoonist named Hoff, whose caption, "Nize baby, eat up all the Post Toasties," was on everyone's lips for months. The cereal was purchased by millions who repeated the humorous phrase to their children.

Post introduced Grape Nuts to the public by offering a one-penny discount coupon good for the purchase of a box of Grape Nuts, thereby starting the "cents-off" practice of modern food merchandising. He quickly learned how to be a capitalist, railing against workers and unions with the same passion that Kellogg devoted to his tirades against the evils of nicotine and alcohol.

MUESLI

Muesli, on the other hand, was not the product of either religious or capitalist zeal, but of a peasant shepherd's simple meal.

The shepherd, so the story goes, was preparing his supper as the last rays of the sun filtered through the Tyrolean peaks in the Swiss Alps. The night before, he had poured fresh milk over a bowl full of coarsely ground whole wheat. Twenty-four hours later the grains had softened and absorbed much of the milk. Over this uncooked porridge he sprinkled nuts, dribbled a large spoonful of honey, and mixed in a cut up, unpeeled apple.

As he was about to dine on this spartan meal, a figure emerged from the woods; a man from the nearby town out on a hike and tired from his walk. The shepherd invited him into his hut to share his dinner with the hiker, who inquired politely about the food and the shepherd's health. He was seventy years old, the shepherd said, never sick a day. Each day he tended his herd, up and down the hills. His breakfast and dinner consisted of this homemade porridge, as did the meals of his neighbors in the area, all of whom were equally healthy.

The hiker was Doctor Bircher-Benner, a world-famous nutritionist and a passionate advocate of a raw (uncooked) diet. Doctor Bircher-Benner's version of the nourishing and delicious cereal was soon served to the patients at his clinic and became their standard breakfast.

Dr. Bircher-Benner introduced Muesli to the non-sheep-tending public in the 1930s, and slowly, by word of mouth, the cereal became popular throughout Europe, reaching the shores of the new world in the 1980s. Although several packaged versions are available, the best kind is the one you can make in your own kitchen. All you need is a package of coarsely ground wheat, fruit, nuts, honey, and milk.

Eternal Life Through Yogurt?

The Biblical patriarch Abraham, so we are told, lived to the advanced age of 175 and was the fountainhead of three great religions: Christianity, Judaism, and Islam. According to one legend, the secret of long life was told to him by an angel: "Eat yogurt!" When told of the birth of his son, Isaac, Abraham offered yogurt to the messengers. Some scholars think the milk in the Biblical phrase "milk and honey," referred to yogurt.

Man cannot live by bread alone; you need yogurt too. Or so thought Pliny the Elder in the first century A.D., when he called yogurt "a good instrument of pleasure."

In the early 1500s the great doctors of Europe were summoned to the bedside of the ailing French monarch, King Francois I. No one could cure him until a Turkish doctor arrived, accompanied by a herd of goats and sheep. He prescribed yogurt for the king, who quickly recovered his health on the new regimen. The doctor returned to Constantinople without revealing the secret of yogurt. The grateful French dubbed yogurt *le lait de la vie éternelle,* the milk of eternal life.

In the early 1900s, news reached Paris of Bulgarian peasants who not only lived to the age of one hundred and beyond, but were even able to have children at those advanced ages. Elie Metchnikoff, a French bacteriologist with the Pasteur Institute and a Nobel Prize-winner, went to Bulgaria to investigate. He observed old men working in the fields, and pausing frequently during the day to eat large bowls of yogurt laced with onions, garlic, nuts, and chopped vegetables.

Convinced that yogurt was responsible for their strength, virility, and long life, Metchnikoff eventually isolated the two strains of yogurt bacteria. One was *Streptococcus thermophilus* and the other, named after the country he found it in, was *Lactobacillus bulgaricus.* Both bacilli manufactured prodigious amounts of B vitamins and attacked an unfriendly virus in the large intestine that Metchnikoff believed produced toxins that hastened aging, senility, and death.

In 1929 Isaac Carasso began selling yogurt commercially in Paris. He named his yogurt *Danone,* after his son Daniel. By the 1950s Carasso had the largest yogurt factory in the world. He set his sights on the United States and opened a plant in New York City, selling yogurt under the Americanized name

Dannon to the ethnic populations of that city. By the mid-sixties Dannon's yogurt began to appeal to a new market: people who wanted to improve their health and who had heard tales of the miracle food.

Today, the yogurt section of supermarkets displays a dazzling array of competing brands, presenting their products in a variety of sizes, flavors, and styles (regular, low-fat, no fat, with fruit, plain, etc.). By the 1980s frozen yogurt stores had opened throughout the country, selling a healthful alternative to ice cream.

Called *kisselo mleko* in Bulgaria, *mazun* in Armenia, *leben* in the Middle East, *dahi* in India, *yaourti* in Greece, and *mast* in Iran, yogurt has spread around the world. In addition to killing the bad virus in the intestine, it offers other benefits. It is easily digested and aids the digestive system in assimilating other foods more effectively. It begins to be absorbed by the body within a half hour, as compared with milk, which takes three to four hours.

Coffee, Hot Chocolate, and Tea

Coffee was introduced into Arabia from Ethiopia in the fifteenth century. According to legend, a goatherd named Kaldi noticed that after his flock ate a certain berry they became frisky. He munched the berries and felt frisky, too. It was years before the Arabs thought to roast the beans and brew them, but eventually coffee evolved as a hot drink. It was just the ticket for the alcohol-abstaining Muslims, who called it their *qahwah,* "wine." (Some sources think the name came from *Kaffa,* in Ethiopia.)

Sweeping through Arabia like a sandstorm, coffee became a daily habit in Mecca, Cairo, Damascus, and Aleppo, then moved to Constantinople where the Turks perfected their unique brewing methods.

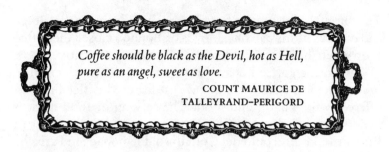

> *Coffee should be black as the Devil, hot as Hell,*
> *pure as an angel, sweet as love.*
>
> COUNT MAURICE DE
> TALLEYRAND–PERIGORD

Coffee was so popular that Sultan Selim I of Persia had his doctors hanged when they had the temerity to suggest he give up his daily cup. From the port of Al Mukha (Mocha) in Yemen coffee plants were taken to Java. From there it migrated to Martinique, Jamaica, and Brazil, where slave labor made it a major crop.

The world's first coffee house opened for business in Constantinople in 1554. In 1650 a Turkish entrepreneur opened a coffee house in Oxford, England. The curious flocked in to taste this delicious brew which refreshed and stimulated the mind and body without the complications of alcohol, particularly its morning-after phenomenon. Not only that, but coffee was alleged to cure all sorts of diseases such as gout, scurvy, consumption, headaches, constipation, and the common cold.

In addition, the gregarious English found the coffee houses rapidly opening around London to be the best of all possible places to meet for conversation and discussion. They soon became gathering places for poets, writers, politicians, and merchants who would sip coffee, trade witticisms, recite poetry, gossip, do business, and plot. King Charles II wanted to close the coffee houses in 1675 because of the conspirators who gathered in them to make trouble; he failed in his effort.

Coffee houses quickly became specialized; certain types of people could be found in one or the other shop. A man named Lloyd had a shop that attracted people in the shipping business.

The shrewd Welshman started a sideline: insuring the ships and cargoes of his patrons. Lloyds of London closed the coffee shop when the insurance business became more lucrative.

When the coffee house was copied on the continent (the first opened in Marseilles in 1671) it featured coffee but also offered wine, liquor, and food. The serving of food made a major advance when the Cafe Procope opened for business in Paris in 1686. Procopio dei Coltelli sold lemonade in Paris for many years. He noted that the cafes in the city where the upper classes went were dull places. The lower class establishments were much more fun to be in, but their wildness and the type of people who frequented them frightened the *bourgeoisie*. He decided to open a place that would be exciting, tasteful, fun to be in, and perfectly safe. He shrewdly chose a location near a famous theater in the rue des Fosses-Saint-Germain (now known as the rue de l'ancienne Comédie). He filled his cafe with large mirrors, expensive chandeliers and real marble tables. In an innovative move, he decorated the room with hundreds of bottles filled with colored water and a display featuring the latest political news.

He sold liqueurs, sherberts, coffee, chocolate, and a wide variety of ice cream, served elegantly in expensive silver dishes. Also available were groceries, jams, perfumes, chocolates, and fruit conserves. The Cafe Procope attracted celebrities. Benjamin Franklin admired the French ladies strolling by as he sipped an aperitif. Napoleon favored the Procope, as did Voltaire, and the doomed revolutionary plotters, Danton and Marat. The Cafe Procope is still in business three hundred years later (try the oysters).

No longer a male-only refuge, the cafes of Europe became the living rooms, dining rooms, and offices for the expanding middle classes, offering anything from a cup of coffee or a snack to a full meal. The atmosphere was informal and you could sit all day without guilt, reading, playing chess, talking, or simply watching the passing parade. Your table was your castle, and you got the bill only when you decided to leave and asked for it. The cafe had entered society.

In 1657, seven years after the first coffee house opened in Oxford, another fad swept England: the first chocolate shop opened in London serving hot chocolate. One of these shops, White's in St. James, eventually became the first private club in England. Hot chocolate, though not destined to take over the role of coffee, nonetheless enjoyed a considerable vogue, particularly for its (undeserved) reputation as an aphrodisiac. After a time, it settled down to being a ladies drink on the continent and for the next two hundred years remained stuck in that role. It slowly found its way into pastries and candies, but it was only in the nineteenth century that it became popular as a candy and in bar form.

While coffee settled in firmly on the continent as the drink of choice, yet another new hot drink was about to make a splash that would have a profound effect on history. Tea had been imported from Japan by the Dutch East India Company since 1610, and this "hay water" was routinely prescribed in Holland for various illnesses. At the same time hot chocolate entered British society, tea also made its appearance, soon eclipsing both coffee and chocolate.

Tea had all the advantages of coffee but didn't hit the stomach, bowels, and heart with the force of coffee and had one advantage that guaranteed success: a housewife could make almost three hundred cups from one pound. "Tee, a China drink," as Samuel Pepys described it, went from a novelty in 1657—known to only a few adventurous gourmets—to the most popular drink in the country within a decade. By 1770 the average Englishman was drinking two pounds a year and eighteen million pounds were imported yearly, three-quarters of it by smugglers. Today the English import almost sixty million pounds a year.

The British love affair with tea made it the hottest commodity in international trade, the cause of the Opium War with China, the impetus for founding enormous tea plantations in India, and the savior of Sri Lanka's economy at the end of the last century when plant disease wiped out that country's coffee crop.

Tea became popular in other parts of the world. The Russians proved to be big tea drinkers, keeping it warm all day in samovars ensconced prominently in their drafty houses; just the thing to keep one warm on a chilly day. In frigid Russia, teacups were bypassed in favor of tall glasses, around which you could get your hands warm while sucking the tea through a cube of sugar held between the teeth. The nomads of Central Asia, on the other hand, ate their tea. They made it very dark, added meal, butter, and cream, and made a mush that was said to ease hunger and thirst simultaneously.

COFFEE STATS

The country that drinks the most coffee *per capita* is not the United States, but Finland, followed by Sweden, Denmark, and Norway. (The United States, however, still consumes more coffee in total than any other country.) Americans consume, per capita, approximately 10 pounds of coffee per year, as compared to .7 pounds of tea. The world's record coffee drinkers are the Finns, who drink 28.3 pounds per year, followed by Sweden with 24.3, Denmark with 23.7, and Norway with 22.4. On a per-cup basis, Americans average two to three cups of coffee per day, compared to Finland, whose citizens keep the cold at bay by downing between six and eight cups each day. Among the developed countries of the world, the lowest per capita consumption of coffee is Ireland, whose inhabitants sip only 3.6 pounds per capita each year, or one cup per day for each citizen, on the average. Except for a small amount of Hawaiian Kona coffee, the United States imports every single bean. The tab for filling the bottomless American cup of java in 1986 was $4,293,000,000.

Soybeans: Feeding a Reluctant World

The versatile soybean was introduced into the United States by Dr. Charles Fearn, an Englishman who discovered it on a trip to China. During World War I he was asked by President Woodrow Wilson to assist the war effort and suggested soybeans as a nourishing substitute for scarce foods.

The health-food movement in the United States was in full swing by this time and welcomed soybeans as a miracle food. Fearn's Soy-O-Pancake Mix was one of the first of many soy products to enter the consumer market through health-food stores.

In the period between the two world wars, soybeans became an important crop in this country, not as a food for humans, but for animals. Today, 95 percent of the United States soybean crop still goes to feed animals. The United States is the world's largest grower of soy beans, producing over two billion bushels in 1986, with a cash value of almost ten billion dollars. The People's Republic of China and Brazil are in second and third place, respectively.

Soybeans have no starch; when cooked they do not soften like other beans, making them difficult to flavor. Cooked whole, soybeans have a gelatinous, slippery texture that most Americans find unpleasant. So, apparently, do consumers in Asia, who never eat the bean whole either. The closest most of us come to eating the whole bean is in soy bean sprouts in salads and Oriental cooking.

Soybeans originated in China over five thousand years ago, and have been a staple food there ever since, spreading throughout Asia in various forms such as tofu, miso, tempeh, and soy sauce (shoyu). Tofu is made of curdled soybeans. (Miso and tempeh are fermented soybeans, and soy sauce is fermented and liquefied soybeans.) Ripe soybeans are prepared by soaking them in water until they swell. Then they are ground up and the mash is allowed to settle. After being strained through a double layer of cheesecloth, the resulting fluid is soy bean milk. The coagulation proceeds with the milk being boiled and then cooled to eighty degrees centigrade. A chemical solution is added to curdle the mix, which is stirred gently with a scoop so the curds which form are not broken down. Sometimes salt is added to speed coagulation. The finished product is tofu, which resembles cottage cheese in form and texture.

When food shortages occurred during World War II, processed soybeans began to be used as a meat extender. Their great advantages are cheapness, extremely high protein content (50 percent), and their bland flavor, which makes them an ideal culinary vehicle for various flavorings. One pound of soy flour cost approximately $1.20 in 1991. Each two-ounce serving contains: 250 calories, 20 grams of protein, 18 grams of complex carbohydrates, 13 grams of dietary fiber, 11 grams of fat, and no salt. This compares favorably with a two-ounce serving of brown rice, which contains: 200 calories, 4 grams of protein, 44 grams of complex carbohydrates, 3.1 grams of fiber, 1 gram of fat, and 5 milligrams of salt.

Soy protein is of the highest type, and is superior to the

protein in all other oil seeds such as safflower, sunflower, rapeseed, and peanuts, making soybeans an ideal extender for meat, poultry, and fish.

In the 1960s and 1970s the American food industry sought to take advantage of these qualities and launched what amounted to a protein revolution. The unmatched technical prowess of American industry, backed by the nearly unlimited ability of American agriculture to produce soybeans, would soon, it was thought, put an end to starvation. Government and industry committees were formed around the world, many under the aegis of the United Nations. Hopes soared. Soybeans were hailed as an inexhaustible resource, the food with a thousand disguises. Every nation could have soy products specifically designed to the needs, tastes, and eating habits of their inhabitants.

One of the biggest tools in the protein revolution was to be meat analogs—soy protein made to look, feel, cook, and taste like meat, chicken, fish, or any other product you might name. This was made possible by an invention in 1954 by R. A. Boyer. Boyer devised a method of spinning soy protein into fibers, similar to the way rayon is made. The fibers were stretched and molded into forms resembling meat, ham, and chicken, and flavored appropriately to suggest the product they imitated. (Boyer had applied modern technology to a process invented by chefs centuries ago in China, when vegetarian Buddhist emperors ordered their cooks to devise meat substitutes. The ingenious cooks obligingly created a series of foods that looked, smelled, and tasted like various meats but were made from mosses, lichen, beans, and other ingredients.)

An important project of the forces of the food revolution, this technique of disguising soy as meat was billed by Albert Spiel, one of the scientists involved, as "The Animal Farm." Many giant food companies poured millions of dollars into the Animal Farm, researching and manufacturing imitation meat, fish, poultry, and many other products—such as rice flour blended with soy protein, then formed in size and shape to imitate rice grains—as well as finding new uses for soy extenders.

The products were tasty, nourishing, and cheap, and promised to do what their creators hoped: abolish hunger worldwide and, at the same time, open huge markets for American soybeans and manufactured products. It would be a textbook example of enlightened capitalism: making a profit on a product that really helped people. Industry was poised to solve the world's hunger problems.

Child-feeding programs were set up using soy mixed into cereal products. Soy milk was used to feed infants in countries where milk (lactose) intolerance was a problem, or where a shortage of nutritional protein existed, indicating a need for protein additives in food. A mixture of corn and soy was developed for use in Central and South America. Soy supplemented with peanut flour and bottled soy protein beverages were marketed in southeast Asia. The United States Food For Peace program was active in assisting food manufacturers to market food products in several countries.

Then came the problems. Cultural habits die hard, and many products met with consumer resistance, even in countries where starvation was a problem. Bureaucratic haggling over the terms of getting the soy products into the various countries arose. It was difficult to find the skilled labor needed to produce soy products in developing countries and many governments were simply not interested in taking money away from other cherished public works projects for something new and untried. Although some progress was made, there were no real success stories and the revolution slowly ground to a halt.

Although the fulfillment of the great promise of soy is yet to come, soy products are slowly finding more acceptance with American consumers. Tofu is still an exotic food but is seen more often in supermarkets, usually in the form of a soft bean curd, ready for any one of a dozen applications in the kitchen. It can be added to soups, fried in combination with a variety of ingredients such as fish and shrimp, mixed into ground meat, or eaten plain. Soy milk and other products are taking their place in the dairy departments of many stores. *Tofutti,* an ice cream made of soybeans, was recently introduced, and has many imitators and a growing following among people who like the taste, are allergic to milk products, are observant of religious dietary laws, or want to cut down on butterfat, with its inherent cholesterol problems, in their diets.

The soy revolution is operating on a delayed fuse. It is an event that is bound to happen, whenever conditions are right and the problems become amenable to solution. Soybeans remain one of the world's most nutritious, abundant, and cheapest sources of high-grade protein; and starvation still stalks the world.

"Don't Forget to Bring the Popcorn, Quadequina"

Popcorn, (popped-corn, to be precise) was discovered five thousand years ago by American Indians. The Indians of the Caribbean invented the popcorn lei, as Christopher Columbus proved when he brought some home for show-and-tell at the court of Ferdinand and Isabella. The Aztecs used popcorn in religious rituals, according to the explorer Cortes, who observed them in Mexico in 1510. Chief Massasoit's brother, Quadequina of the Wampanoag tribe, brought a few skin bags filled with popped corn as his contribution to the party when the Pilgrims invited them to Thanksgiving dinner in 1621.

The Indians at first held an ear of corn over the fire until the kernels popped. Later, they learned to first remove the kernels, throw them into the fire, and scramble for the ones that popped free. Finally, they heated sand in a clay pot, covered the seeds with hot sand and fished the popped corn out of the sand.

Popcorn pops because it contains water which turns into

steam when heated. The kernel's skin is so strong that the steam cannot escape. When enough trapped steam has built up, the kernel explodes into a soft, white mass. There must be at least fourteen percent moisture for it to pop. Those with twelve percent or less pop partially or not at all. Unpopped kernels, once called *old maids,* are now called *duds* (unexploded bombs).

Seeking to develop large and fluffy popcorn with a low percentage of duds, two agronomists, Charles Bowman and Orville Redenbacher, succeeded in 1952. The companies that sold popcorn weren't interested because the new strain cost too much to produce and would raise the price over what the market would bear—or so they thought.

Orville was so convinced the public would buy his new popcorn that he packaged and distributed it himself. His faith was justified a few years later when his popcorn became the nation's number one in sales. Today, over 190,000,000 pounds of popcorn are eaten in the United States annually. The average American popcorn-eater consumes two pounds a year.

A Potato Chip on His Shoulder

"The customer wants his french-fries sliced thinner; says they're too thick." The cook stared sullenly at the head-waiter, mumbled something under his breath and returned shortly with another platter of potatoes. "Still too thick," was the report. "He says if you can't make 'em thinner you ain't much of a cook."

The furious cook took a razor-sharp knife and cut a batch of potatoes so thin you could read a newspaper through them. Frying them to a crisp, golden-brown he handed them to the waiter. "Let's see if he can get a fork into these," he growled.

As he peered out through the round window in the swinging door to the dining room, he beheld an amazing sight. Not only did the customer like them, but diners at surrounding tables were converging to sample the chips.

It happened at Moon Lake Lodge in Saratoga Springs, New York, in 1853. The cook was George Crum, an American Indian credited with inventing America's most popular snack food. They were called Saratoga Chips and their success emboldened Crum to open his own restaurant.

A Prize in Every Box

Stories abound in the food industry of the United States about poor immigrants who, just off the boat and with no real skills, bought a pushcart with their last dollars and later entered food history as the founder of a chain of markets, an inventor of a device that made food cheaply, a person who created a new kind of food, or a new way of presenting an old food.

Such a story was that of a German immigrant, F. W. Rueckheim, who got a job on a farm in Illinois. Rueckheim eventually saved two hundred dollars and invested it in a popcorn stand in Chicago in 1871. He slowly added new items to his stand such as marshmallows, caramel candy, and peanuts. When he added molasses taffy to his inventory, inspiration struck.

His customers seemed to favor peanuts, popcorn, and molasses taffy more than his other wares. If he combined them in one product, he reasoned, they would love it all the more. He called the new candy Cracker Jack, reportedly because a friend made the exclamation after he tasted it. (*Cracker jack* was a slang expression in those days, meaning "something very pleasing.")

It was not long after the creation of the candy that a prize was put into every box. The sailor boy on the box and his dog, Bingo, were modeled after Rueckheim's grandson, who died when he was eight years old. The image of the little boy on the Cracker Jack box was carved on his loving grandfather's tombstone when he died.

The Misunderstood Pretzel

Popcorn and potato chips were given to the world by American Indians. They are also rather noisy foods: popcorn, whose very name indicates its sonic nature, and potato chips, which make noise when eaten and whose acoustical properties have been exploited by chip manufacturers and their advertising minions to great advantage.

Pretzels make some noise when eaten, but that has never been their claim to fame. They are not as popular a snack food as they once were: few people order a bag of pretzels to eat in the movies. Perhaps the reason is the visible salt, now out of favor, or maybe it's the skinny appearance of most packaged pretzels, whose taste leaves something to be desired. They don't fill you up the way a bucket of popcorn does, or have the oily, satisfying taste of potato chips, and their high salt content and dry texture build a powerful thirst. They can be found in little plastic dishes on bar counters, and have even been challenged in those emporiums by such odd snack foods as goldfish crackers and others of unknown contents made to resemble nuts.

The real reason, perhaps, is that pretzels are no longer what they were. The dessicated pretzels in the supermarkets are a far cry from the original pretzels, which should be large, soft, and chewy, and should be eaten freshly baked and hot. Perhaps the last, great outpost in the New World for pretzels is Philadelphia. They are sold by street vendors who keep them hot in glass enclosures on their pushcarts and serve them with a special mustard.

The pretzel comes not from Germany, as you might guess, but from Italy. The Italian word for pretzel, *bracciatelli,* means "folded arms," a reference to its shape. According to legend, the pretzel was invented by a monk in Northern Italy in 1610, who baked pretzels in the shape of folded praying arms as prizes for his students who recited their catechism without error.

In parts of Europe pretzels are a Lenten food. Although the

pretzel has no particular religious significance, their priestly origin in Europe and their resemblance to arms crossed in a prayerful attitude made them a natural. Special vendors appear in the streets on Ash Wednesday and hawk pretzels to the pious until the Easter season is done. They appear in countless Medieval illuminations and drawings.

During the early sixteenth century Vienna was besieged by the Turks who, unable to scale the wall surrounding the city, decided to tunnel under it. They were heard digging during the middle of the night by pretzel bakers who were working through the night preparing their next day's wares. The bakers alerted the troops and the attempt was foiled. To this day the European symbol for bakers is a pretzel.

Glorious Ice Cream

> *As cold waters to a thirsty soul,*
> *So is good news from a far country.*
>
> The Book of Proverbs, The Hezekiah Collection

Some form of ice cream or flavored ices has been part of civilized life since King Solomon cooled his pronouncements with chilled drinks.

Alexander the Great had trenches dug and filled with ice brought down from the mountains by runners, to cool his wine while he waited to attack an enemy. Wine-flavored ices, which Alexander certainly must have known, were the ancestors of today's sherberts and wine coolers, and were known to the early Jews, Greeks, and Romans. So popular were they that Hippocrates, the father of medicine, complained that "most men would rather run the hazard of their lives or health [by drinking cold drinks in hot weather] than be deprived of the pleasure of drinking out of ice."

Among the curiosities brought back from Cathay by Marco Polo was a recipe for a concoction made from ice, milk, and fruit flavors, big news to the Italians of the Renaissance, who had forgotten everything about their historic heritage of cooled ices in the thousand-year sleep of the Dark and Middle Ages. The Italians soon developed *gelato,* the precursor of modern ice cream, from this primitive recipe.

The frozen dessert was brought to France by the fourteen-year-old Catherine de Medici in 1533, when she married the Duke of Orleans. A French chef brought the secret formula for ice cream to England early in the 17th century. He was hired by Charles I, who so loved ice cream that he gave a pension of twenty pounds sterling to the chef, on condition he keep the formula secret. When the King died in 1649 the chef was freed of his obligation and quickly sold out to a consortium of noblemen. The secret was out. So popular was ice cream in Europe that Beethoven complained in 1794, "It will soon be impossible to have any ice cream, for as winter is mild, ice is rare."

Ice cream migrated to America before the Revolution. The frozen indulgences of George Washington, Alexander Hamilton, Thomas Jefferson, and James and Dolley Madison are well-documented. To celebrate his victory at the Battle of Fallen Timbers in 1789, General "Mad Anthony" Wayne served his men ice cream, "Which the army has not seen since it left the east."

When ice cream was introduced in France in 1677, the French immediately began creating new ways to serve this delicious dessert. Over the years they developed the *bombe,* made in a round (bomb-shaped) metal mold; *coupes glacées,* several scoops of ice cream served with fruit and *créme Chantilly,* (whipped cream flavored with vanilla); *mousses,* and *parfaits.* One of the most unusual and innovative ice cream dishes was *omelette à la Norvegiènne,* a log of ice cream wrapped in a stiff meringue, quickly browned in the oven and served immediately. It was named after the Scandinavian country because Norway was the principle distributor of ice in Europe in those pre–ice machine days. When the dessert was introduced to America in the mid-eighteen-hundreds, nationalistic chefs rechristened it "Baked Alaska," after the coldest place they knew.

The chocolate sundae was once sold only on Sunday. An ice cream parlor customer named George Hallauer invented it spontaneously one Sunday during the Gay Nineties. "Sucking sodas" was tolerated—barely—in some communities, but was considered coarse. Indulging this vulgarity on Sunday, the Lord's day, was simply out of the question. The sundae became the perfect treat for those who craved ice cream on Sunday but did not want to offend their pious neighbors. The word was purposely misspelled so as to not give the impression of mocking the Lord's day.

The hot fudge sundae, an improvement on the Gay Nineties original, was invented by an unsung soda jerk at C. C. Brown's ice cream parlor in Los Angeles, California, in 1906. The refreshing combination of hot and cold sensations is still being served at Brown's, now something of a historic monument to ice cream buffs visiting Hollywood.

Upon arrival at Ellis Island in 1921, immigrants were given ice cream, a food typical of America, according to the superintendent of the island. Puzzled, many of them spread this frozen butter on bread before eating it. In the 1920s, Paul S. Crawley opened an ice cream parlor in Shanghai and sold over one million Eskimo Pies in the first year of operation.

Hollywood got into the act when Eddie Cantor made a movie, *Kid Millions*, featuring a fantasy ice cream dance extravaganza. Hollywood starlets were photographed licking ice cream cones, and dozens of boy-meets-girl movies featured scenes of smitten teen-aged lovers flirting over banana splits.

The Mel-O-Roll, popular during the forties, was a cylinder of sweet vanilla, or lightly flavored pale-chocolate ice cream wrapped in yellow paper and served in a cone made to fit the cylindrical shape. The customer would carefully unwrap the paper, use it to press the roll firmly into the cone, lick the remnants of ice cream off the paper, and discard it. The idea was to give the impression of ice cream so pure and fresh it was served still in its wrapper, an alternative to the unstable cone, which was prone to lose its contents if not properly packed. Each Mel-O-Roll contained exactly the same amount of ice cream as all the others, unlike hand-packed scoops. Mel-O-Rolls had a creamy flavor and a devoted following until they disappeared from the market after World War II.

The Dixie Cup, once tremendously popular, is still around today, but now refers to a generic paper cup with a disposable top held in place by an indented depression and removed with a small tab. The original contained an equal amount of chocolate and vanilla ice cream packed side-by-side. The top had a picture of a movie star on the round, inside surface. The photograph was separated from the ice cream by a waxed paper membrane that was peeled off by the customer (after first licking off the ice cream coating the lid); it was part of the ritual of buying the Dixie Cups. Children invariably ate the chocolate ice cream down to the bottom first, then the vanilla (a tradition echoed in Oreo cookies).

The neighborhood ice cream truck was once a familiar feature of the American landscape, with its merry chimes and throngs of clamoring children clutching a few coins carefully wrapped in paper to survive the flight from a third story window. First there was the Eskimo Pie, also called the I Scream Bar. The problem was that the ice cream would melt and become messy.

In 1920 Harry Burt, Sr., who believed that the mind's "humours" were affected by what one ate—a throwback to Medieval beliefs—took the concept of the ice cream bar one step further by inserting a stick into it, thus allowing the ice cream to be eaten without melting all over the hand.

The Good Humors man in his gleaming white truck was always dressed in clean, white linens and the company prided itself on wholesome ingredients prepared in sanitary plants. Burt ran his show like a military operation, complete with uniforms, ranks, and a manual of behavior. It was an impressive operation in those days of casual merchandising, and a model of what was to come when the age of fast food dawned a half-century later. Mothers who would not permit their children to buy from other vendors had no qualms about the Good Humors man.

If you got a Good Humors bar whose stick was imprinted with the name of the company (you had to eat the ice cream off the stick to find out) you got another bar free. The company was generous and there was always someone in the neighborhood who won a free bar. "Lucky" Good Humors sticks have recently resurfaced as collectibles, commanding hefty prices.

During World War II, airmen placed ice cream mix in large containers and put them in the tail-gunner's cockpit before leaving on a mission. When they returned, the freezing air and the vibration of the plane had made a fine ice cream with which to celebrate a successful sortie.

Ice cream brings out the best in people. Associated with milk, a pure and basic food, its sweet cooling taste has pleased emperors and kings throughout history, and is today an inexpensive way of obtaining ten minutes of cool bliss for anyone who can afford a cone. Prices have skyrocketed from the ten cent cone of the Depression, but even at the 1991 price of $1.50 for a gourmet scoop, ice cream is still the cheapest luxury food available.

Chapter 4

Of Food, Mind, and Body

No man can be wise on an empty stomach.

George Eliot

The body is organized much like a large, modern corporation. There are a variety of systems which are assigned different tasks: internal delivery systems and transportation networks; an internal communication network to get information around the system easily; a commissary for providing nourishment to the employees; a network of supervisors who report to department managers, who report in turn to various directors; and a chief executive officer (C.E.O.), who runs the entire system to accomplish the goals of the enterprise.

Like most modern corporations, Body, Inc. is located in a vertical structure, complete with entrances and exits to interface with the outer world, and a penthouse where the view is best. There the resemblance ends. Unlike a modern corporation, Body, Inc. is mobile, and the entire structure can be moved at will, instantly, for any reason. As in the world of business, the C.E.O. is located in the penthouse suite, somewhere inside the computer room, which is surrounded by protective armor plate. Important information receptors are nearby, such as the eyes, ears, nose, and throat, feeding data directly into the computer.

The C.E.O., who gets the credit for running the enterprise, is not a "hands-on" administrator; the staff runs the systems according to a reliable program installed long ago. The C.E.O. takes orders from a still higher—or, in this case, lower—authority. The chairman of the board, whose office is located in the bowels of the structure, is blind and deaf, but can speak, loudly and clearly, when the system is threatened. It is the stomach which really controls the mind and the body, letting them amuse themselves however they please once their basic job is done.

"Feed me!" it shouts. "Feed me, feed me, feed me!"

Feeding the Appetite for Sex

> *The member of Abou el Heiloukh remained erect for*
> *thirty days without a break,*
> *because he did eat onions.*
> The Perfumed Garden
> Shaykh Nefawzi

Aphrodisiacal food is like astrology: both go back to the beginning of civilization and both have often been debunked. And yet . . .

Some people swear there are such things, citing first-hand experience. Could it be our old friend the placebo, working in an overheated environment to make our dreams come true? Or could there really be hard evidence in all those old-husband's tales? Modern medicine has chemicals that will stimulate sex; why not food?

Research seems to indicate a physiological relationship between the enjoyment of eating and the enjoyment of sex. A study at State University of New York's State Medical Center found that women who enjoy food seem able to enjoy sex more than women who don't; a positive attitude towards food indicated a similarly positive attitude towards sex. The pressure from society in America, however, is the reverse, as some researchers proved at Lafayette College in Easton, Pennsylvania.

They surveyed one hundred men who watched women eat four meals, from a small salad accompanied by a glass of plain soda water, to a huge submarine sandwich, two side dishes, a large soda and a big piece of chocolate cake. The men in the survey said that women who ordered small meals and then nibbled on them were more feminine and likable than those who ordered large meals and ate with gusto. The pressure to be slim that is exerted by male society clashes with the natural gusto of women who love life and love to eat and make love. It's enough to drive you to the refrigerator. To further complicate the issue, slim and beautiful actress Audrey Hepburn was asked recently how she managed to stay so slim. Her answer: "I eat a lot."

Proponents of the you–can–never–be–too–thin school of eating should be given pause by a study by Dr. William Shipman and Dr. Ronald A. Schwartz, clinical psychologists in Chicago, who learned that heavier–than–average women have sex more often than women of average weight. Their study revealed that women of average weight have sex 8.6 times a month, while overweight women have sex 11.9 times a month. The sex act burns up two hundred plus calories—worth remembering as you reach for a second helping of dessert.

A study of food aphrodisiacs, however, quickly leads to the ridiculous. Almost every fruit and vegetable and everything related to them (including garden dirt) has been thought to be a sexual stimulant by one or another civilization—usually because the shape, texture, or color of the object resembled genitalia, such as eggplant, horseradish, oysters, and peaches.

Apicius, the Roman cookbook writer, had recipes for laggard lovers. Poets, historians, and philosophers such as Homer, Ovid, Martial, Aristotle, and Pliny sang hallelujahs to the greater glory of Aphrodite and her namesakes, and also to the stimulating power of onions.

Emperor Nero ate so many leeks to improve his prowess that he was called *porrophagus* (leek-eater) behind his back. In India, garlic mixed with lard and rubbed on the penis was said to increase sexuality. Whether it was the garlic or the application process that provided the stimulus is debatable. At certain times in India, garlic, onions, and beans were thought to be so stimulative that they were banned.

Claims for onion and garlic potency are made to the present day, but there is some sentiment that the fragrant lily peters out in the bedroom and becomes a *counter*-aphrodisiac due to the unpleasant odors. If you wish to experiment with onions and garlic aphrodisiacs, do so with a consenting partner. Even better, if your partner in this experiment consumes the same amount of onions or garlic that you do, the unpleasant odors will cancel themselves out.

Flowers have been used as aphrodisiacs for centuries. Their beautiful shapes and colors, and their fragrant odors have naturally suggested sex to many, and perhaps the thought alone put some in the mood for love. Henry VIII, whose appetite is legendary, had candied roses, primroses, violets, and hawthorn at many meals. Belladonna has been used to make the eyes more attractive (they enlarge the pupils), and narcissus is a much-favored sex stimulant.

Experimenters should purchase edible flowers from a reliable store or herbalist to avoid flowers with pesticides on them. Many flowers are not harmless, and experimenting without professional guidance could lead to trouble from poisonous blossoms, leaves, or berries. Edible flowers usually have a pleasant taste, and many are quite nutritious, attributes which may account for their recent revival as a specialty food. The list of aphrodisiacal flowers runs into well over a hundred names, many of them difficult to obtain. Here's a selection:

Anemone, artemisa, caperberry, cereus, chrysanthemum, crocus, cyclamen, dahlia, dandelion, dragon's blood, fleawort, frankincense, fuchsia, grass, hashish, henna, hyssop, jasmine, jimsonweed, juniper, laurel, lavender, lilac, lotus, maidenhair, mallows, marijuana, myrrh, myrtle, orchid, palmito, pansy, peony, periwinkle, poppies, rocket, roses, sarsaparilla, sassafras, saw palmetto, snakeroot, thistle, tobacco, tulips, verbena, violet, water lily, yohimbe.

The Greeks called the carrot *philtron* and noted its resemblance to the penis. They made endless concoctions called *philtres* to stimulate their ardor. The term survived into Medieval times as *philter,* a love-potion, and is with us today as *filter,* with a different meaning.

Greek and Roman aphrodisiacs were minor league compared to what went on during the Middle Ages. Wizards, witches, alchemists, and sorcerers plied their trade to a willing and gullible clientele from royalty to peasants. A repressive society with an ignorant population and an all-powerful ruling class and clergy didn't match the Saturnalias and orgies of earlier civilizations, but what they lacked in permissiveness they more than made up for in the imagination of their concoctions.

A maiden was instructed to sit naked in a tub of wheat, moving the grains so as many as possible came in contact with her genitalia. The wheat was then ground and baked and the bread was fed to the man she desired. In another version, a nude woman knelt while a loaf of bread was kneaded on her buttocks. The bread baked from this dough was guaranteed to inflame the passions of any man who ate it.

Some of the exotic ingredients used in Medieval aphrodisiacs can scarcely be considered food for the body, but apparently they did work to stimulate the mind. Some were difficult to obtain—like alligator semen—and even more difficult to administer to an unsuspecting lover; others were so disgusting that it became an exercise of mind over matter. Pubic hair was a favorite, burned to ash and mixed into bread dough or liquid. Menstrual blood, preferably from a virgin, was another popular ingredient as were other expendable body products such as nail clippings, urine, and perspiration.

Dining in the nude was a popular form of arousal throughout history, from the Egyptians, Greeks, Romans, and through the Middle Ages. Some Medieval sex feasts apparently required quite complex preparations. In one illustration dating from late fifteenth-century Germany, seven or eight wooden tubs large enough for two people are lined up next to each other on a raised, curtained dais with a man and woman in each tub facing each other, wearing nothing except their hats and jewelry. A long board with tablecloth has been laid down the length of the tubs, separating them into two sections. The dozen people in the tubs are feasting as they bathe, and one couple has proceeded beyond dining to whatever heavy petting was called in those days. In the background the goings-on are watched by two men, one apparently a priest or high official, and the other with crown, scepter, and ermine collar: a king. A minstrel serenades the diners with a lute while a pet dog frolics. Off to a side another couple, finished with dinner, proceed to the bedroom to consummate their passion.

The Duc de Richelieu, a contemporary of Casanova and nephew of the famed Cardinal, was noted for his elaborate nude meals in which everyone from mistresses to titled ladies dined in the buff on oysters and marzipan, considered aphrodisiacs. Another contemporary, Field Marshall Soubise, invited only women to his little soirees; ladies fought for the honor of dining unclad with the Field Marshall. Mademoiselle Dubois, an actress and one of Soubise's favorite dinner guests, kept an account of every coupling she had over a ten year period. The total came to 16,527, or four and a half per day on average. Food and sex have always stimulated each other.

Bull's testicles were served during the Gay Nineties in San Francisco restaurants such as the Maison Doree and the Poodle Dog (which also thoughtfully provided private bedrooms for their satisfied clientele). Bull's testicles contain testosterone, the male hormone; the gourmets of a hundred years ago who ate them with such zest, lasciviously twirling their moustachios, may have been on to something.

The key to aphrodisiacal food throughout history has been its role in sparking anticipation, a necessary prerequisite to still the distractions of life and allow the mind and body to be released to the powerful, suppressed impulses of the reproductive system. The power of aphrodisiacal food, like beauty, is in the eye of the beholder.

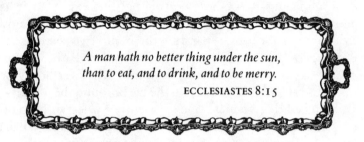

A man hath no better thing under the sun, than to eat, and to drink, and to be merry.

ECCLESIASTES 8:15

Ah, Sweet Mystery of Love!

Chocolate too has been considered an aphrodisiac. It is no coincidence that some chocolate candy comes in heart-shaped boxes and one type is called a Kiss.

Aztec Emperor Moctezuma II drank fifty glasses of chocolate sweetened with honey every day and an extra goblet or two before sex. The Spaniards, generally scornful of Aztec practices, tried the delicious brew themselves but left no record of its effect on their prowess.

So intrigued were they with this odd, satisfying drink that they began to study its secrets in the mid-1500s. Four hundred years later scientists are still trying to fathom the mystery of chocolate. Although they have learned much, they are far from their goal.

Why does African chocolate taste different than Asian-grown chocolate? Why is some chocolate more intense than others? Can the intensity be controlled? One problem is that taste and intensity are subjective, impossible to measure in a laboratory. Only tasters can tell the difference between chocolates.

What is known is that chocolate originated in the Amazon basin and grows only in an area bounded by twenty degrees latitude on both sides of the equator. Thirty-five countries grow it as a cash crop. The botanical name for it is *Theobroma cacao,* "the food of the gods."

The cacao tree grows pods containing a tasty, pulpy fruit embedded with beans. These are fermented for a week, roasted, hulled, and ground down to the nib, the heart of the bean, which contains 54 percent cocoa butter. Cocoa butter fat is removed by further grinding in a process invented by a Dutchman named C.J. Van Houten in the 1800s (a process also used in cosmetics and leather tanning). Yet another process brings to it the rich, familiar chocolate color, and finally the powder is ready for the confectioner's artistry.

Dark (bittersweet) chocolate contains little or no cocoa butter or milk fat. Milk chocolate contains powdered milk and cocoa butter. In pure form, chocolate is nutritious and actually good for you. Three and a half ounces of Hershey's cocoa contains 27.3 grams of protein, 12.8 grams of fat, 45.7 grams of carbohydrates, 20 milligrams of sodium, and important amounts of calcium, phosphorous, iron, potassium, magnesium, copper, zinc, manganese, and vitamin A.

What makes it fattening and bad for the body is not the chocolate, but what is put into it as it is processed into candy, chocolate syrup, cocoa powder and all of its other delightful forms. Cocoa butter, sugar, salt, nuts, and saturated fats are the villains.

It is true that there is caffeine in chocolate as in coffee. But twelve ounces of hot chocolate contains only 17.5 milligrams of caffeine compared to 100 to 200 milligrams in an equal quantity of coffee. Chocolate also contains theobromine, a chemical similar to caffeine. Unlike caffeine, it is not considered by some experts as a stimulant, but seems to have the opposite effect of relaxing the body.

Contrary to legend, chocolate is not able to sexually arouse the human animal. It may well, however, put you in the mood—one sensual pleasure leading to another. Some researchers argue that this mood-changing effect is credited to

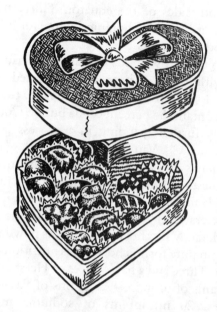

another chemical, phenylethylamine (PEA), which puts the chocolate-eater into a euphoric state of mind some have compared to the feeling of being in love. On the other hand, both sausage and cheese contain one hundred times more PEA than chocolate, and few of us have tried to melt the heart of the one we love by a heart-shaped assortment of salami and longhorn cheddar. (On the subject of melting, cocoa butter melts at body temperature, which is why a bar of chocolate is not a good thing to keep in your pocket. During Operation Desert Storm in Saudi Arabia a chocolate bar was developed using a fat that melts at much higher temperatures, enabling the troops to have their chocolate and eat it, too.)

Modern chemistry and genetic research is turning its big guns on chocolate, trying to uncover the mystery. Perhaps the enjoyment of chocolate is—like the enjoyment of a magician's performance—something we should simply accept and not question.

The Romans Should Have Got the Lead Out

The decline and fall of the Roman Empire was caused by a complex combination of political, social and military factors. New evidence, however, suggests perhaps another reason: it may have been something they ate. Tombs of important Romans from around 150 B.C. contain bones with unusually high levels of lead.

The periodic table of elements shows lead abbreviated as Pb, derived from the Latin word for lead, *plumbum*. The English words *plumbing* and *plumb line* come from the Latin root. Roman aqueducts brought water from miles away and channeled it into private homes using ingenious systems unrivaled even today in many countries. They used lead extensively in their plumbing systems. Senators sipped water to cool their rhetoric—water that poured forth from lead pipes. Women's cosmetics contained lead, and wine was sweetened with syrup that had been boiled in lead-lined pots. Every time a high-born Roman drank wine (several times a day, for many), lead dissolved in the wine was ingested.

Greeks enslaved by the Romans introduced them to *calderiums,* pots lined with lead that masked the unpleasant, coppery taste of food and drink prepared in bronze containers. It became all the rage. No Roman household permitted food to be served unless it was cooked in a *calderium.*

Symptoms of lead poisoning include sterility and general weakness, apathy, mental retardation and impairment, and early death. Could it be that the greatest empire the world has ever known was brought to its knees by an inadvertent toxic food additive?

An Onion a Day Keeps the Doctor Away

If you want to kill the germs in your mouth you can do so without mouthwash; eat onions. Chewing raw onions for five minutes kills *all* the germs in the mouth, making it sterile; a good thing to know next time you get a cold. According to researchers in the United States and India, onions also kill the germs that cause tooth decay.

Onions contain iron, calcium, potassium, protein, and vitamins B and C. One medium sized onion contains only thirty-eight calories and as much vitamin C as two apples, one banana, one tomato, or one orange. Onions are among the ten most popular vegetables in the country. They were named by *Prevention Magazine* as one of twenty-five superfoods that can help combat heart disease and cancer.

During an outbreak of infectious fever in London in the early 1800s, French priests (who ate onions and garlic regularly) ministered to the sick and dying and suffered no ill effects, while many English clergymen (who never ate onions or garlic) became ill and died. Alexander the Great, General Ulysses Grant, and General George Patton all insisted on onions for their soldiers. Captain Cook made his men eat them to avoid scurvy. In World War I and II, garlic was used to treat gangrene.

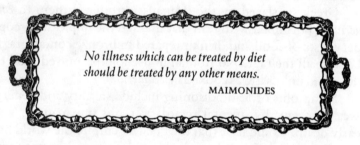

No illness which can be treated by diet should be treated by any other means.
MAIMONIDES

The Strange Case of Les Quatres Voleurs

A pestilence swept through Marseilles in 1721, killing thousands of people. Four criminals scheduled to die were made to bury the dead, on the theory that since they were going to die anyway, *pourquoi pas?* The four thieves not only did not die from the plague but seemed to thrive. The authorities became curious. They learned that the thieves were drinking wine in which garlic was soaked until it became pulpy. While the ultimate fate of the four is unknown, their invention, *vinaigre des quatre voleurs,* "Four Thieves Vinegar," may still be purchased in France today. True stories such as this contribute to the centuries-old reputation of garlic (and onions) as an aid to good health and a cure for disease.

Fruit of the Wine

My first wife drove me to drink.
I shall always be grateful to her for that.
    W. C. Fields

"I'll have a glass of chablis, please," the diner politely instructs the waiter, under the illusion that white wine helps maintain a slim figure. Wine is not a diet drink. A pint and a half of *vin ordinaire* has the calories of a quart of milk, two pounds of potatoes, or a one-pound loaf of bread. It is a food of sorts, which is why winos, who generally don't have the best eating habits, don't starve to death (although they may drink themselves there): they get their calories in liquid form.

Another misconception we should banish from the table is that there is a difference between cooking wine and drinking wine; there is only bad wine, good wine, and great wine. Good wine improves the flavor of food; bad wine doesn't. Great wine shouldn't be used in cooking because the qualities that make it great disappear with heat. Any ordinary, good wine is fine for cooking.

As you thoughtfully gaze into the ruby reflections in your wine glass and slowly sip the rich, lush liquid, do you sometimes wonder if you are driving another nail into your coffin, or, on the other hand, do you congratulate yourself on adding years to your life and improving your health with an occasional glass of the fruit of the vine? The answer depends on whether you ask the question of your doctor or your government.

Dr. R. Curtis Ellison, chief of preventive medicine and epidemiology at the Boston University School of Medicine, says: "If there were no alcoholism, no toxic effects . . . we'd be starting our children with a bit of wine. The evidence is very striking that moderate alcohol consumption has a beneficial effect."

The United States federal government couldn't disagree more. In a publication entitled, "Dietary Guidelines for Americans," the government states its position: "Drinking . . . has no net benefit, is linked with many health problems, is the cause of many accidents and can lead to addiction." Your government doesn't want you to drink and says that consumption of alcohol is not recommended.

With a half-million Americans dying from heart attacks each year and one out of every ten an alcoholic, the problem is very real. Alcoholism is a particularly devastating killer, not only destroying the life of the victim, but tearing families apart, making neurotics of children, and killing innocent victims in automobile accidents.

Per capita consumption of beer in the United States is 34.4 gallons; wine is 3.4 gallons, and distilled spirits 2.3 gallons (1987). Almost half of the price of a bottle of distilled spirits goes to the government. Of an eighty-proof bottle containing 750 ml of spirits which sells for an average price of $7.13, $1.67 (23.7 percent of the total price) goes to federal tax, $1.48 (20.7 percent) goes to state and local taxes, and the rest, $3.98 (55.6 percent) covers all other costs, including contents, bottling, advertising, distribution, etc.

In 1983 the taxes paid to federal, state, and local governments from the sale of distilled spirits in the United States amounted to almost seven billion dollars. In 1984 the United

States imported 223.3 million gallons of malt liquor (beer, ale, etc.), of which 37 percent came from the Netherlands, 27 percent from Canada, and 16 percent from the (then) Republic of West Germany. Eight out of ten bottles of imported beer come from those three countries.

The highest alcohol consumption per capita in the United States is in the west, plus Wisconsin and Florida, with the exception of Utah, which has the lowest per capita consumption at 1.73 gallons. The southern and central states have the least amount per capita.

Here are some advantages and disadvantages of alcohol consumption—you decide. But first, some definitions:

Moderate drinker: one or two drinks a day.

Heavy drinker: three or more drinks a day.

A drink: five ounces of wine, twelve ounces of beer, one ounce of whisky (or other liquor of equal proof).

ADVANTAGES OF MODERATE ALCOHOLIC CONSUMPTION

- Seems to decrease risk of heart disease. Moderate drinkers have 20 percent less coronary disease–related deaths than abstainers or heavy drinkers.
- Relaxes the mind and body and stimulates the appetite; does not seem to be a factor in causing obesity.
- Decreases incidence of gallstones.
- The tannin in red wines helps inhibit blood clotting that leads to heart attacks, and is thought to stimulate the beneficial high density lipoproteins (HDL) while simultaneously reducing the cholesterol level. Quercetin, a chemical compound that acts to block the activity of cancerous cells, has been found in red grapes (and also in onions and yellow squash).
- Wine can add variety to a restricted diet and make food more palatable.

DISADVANTAGES OF MODERATE ALCOHOLIC CONSUMPTION

- With the consumption of two drinks per day for women, or four for men, the incidence of cirrhosis of the liver increases markedly.
- Two drinks (or more) per day will elevate blood pressure and increase risk of coronary disease.
- Four or more drinks a day may cause heart disease, stroke, as well as cancer of the mouth and stomach. Children of drinking mothers may have congenital physical and mental deficiencies.
- Some studies link increases in breast cancer among women with moderate drinking habits.
- Abstainers and those prone to substance abuse run greater risks to their health and the dangers of alcoholism than others.

"The data shows moderate wine drinkers live longer, are healthier, and age in a better way," says the chairman of the department of medicine at Pacific Presbyterian Medical Center in San Francisco, Dr. Keith Marton. "Hints throughout medical literature always favor wine drinkers," he added. He agrees that heavy consumption of alcohol among women will increase the risk of birth defects as much as 10 percent, but says no studies have been made of women who consume three or less drinks per day.

It is difficult to accuse impartial medical evidence of sexism, but studies show that women are less tolerant of alcohol than men and run greater risks from steady consumption of alcohol, even in moderation. The ideal profile, according to the studies, of someone likely to benefit from moderate alcoholic consumption is a middle-aged male who exercises on a regular basis, drinks on an even pattern, and has a cholesterol count of two hundred or higher.

You should stay away from alcohol completely if you are pregnant (or trying to be), drive a vehicle, take medication regularly, cannot tolerate alcohol or have a history of alcoholism, or are underage (adolescent or younger). If you drink because it's part of your dietary regimen, alcohol is a food. If you drink to benefit your heart (or state of mind), it's a drug.

The argument for wine as the drink of preference is a strong one. In addition to its long history (with beer) as part of most civilizations going back to the dawn of history, studies at Washington University in St. Louis, Missouri, find that the majority of wine drinkers are moderate and responsible people, who average three to four glasses a week, and not more than one and a half glasses at a time.

According to the *Journal of Substance Abuse,* 75 percent of wine consumption is done in a home environment, with 82 percent of the consuming done within the framework of a meal. The Department of Justice chimes in with the finding that only 2 percent of drunk driving arrests involve wine (1988 report). There's a reason for this: ethanol (the alcohol in wine) is absorbed more slowly into the bloodstream because of the presence of tannins in wine, and also due to the buffering effect of the food usually eaten at the same time.

Drinking wine and other alcoholic beverages is good for you and it's bad for you; it can make you healthier and it can ruin your health; it can make you live longer and it can kill you before your time; it can cause disease and it can cure, or alleviate disease; it is a social habit and it is an anti-social habit.

It's enough to drive you to drink.

Food as Medicine

Good news for committed grazers: paranoia, schizophrenia, depression, allergy, hypoglycemia, and other diseases affecting the mind and body can often be cured by food.

Called ortho-molecular medicine by one of its pioneers, the treatment aims to alter the chemical balance of the body by adding (or subtracting) the offending food, or using megadoses of vitamins and minerals.

During World War II, paranoids and schizophrenics in Greece, deprived of bread because of food shortages under the Nazi regime, showed improvement in their condition. Some patients have been cured of deafness by eliminating tomatoes from their diet. Hyperactivity in children was cured in some cases by eliminating bottled cola drinks or sugared doughnuts from their diets and substituting more wholesome foods.

Throughout history food has been the medicine of first resort. The ancient Egyptians prescribed various foods as medicine, such as onions and garlic, and used honey as a dressing on wounds, to prevent infection and nourish new tissue growth. Roman doctors sterilized wounds with wine. As recently as World War II, doctors in the field used onion or garlic juice as an antiseptic when supplies of regular medicines ran out.

There are even a few magic bullets in the plant kingdom: foods which, by themselves, will cure certain diseases. For example, adding oranges or other citrus fruit to a diet will cure scurvy. Magic bullets (sometimes called wonder drugs) are the exception rather than the rule. Most foods containing substances that alleviate disease either do not contain enough of the substance to cure a specific disease unless the food is taken in enormous and unrealistic quantities, or contain other substances whose presence in the same food can be threatening and do harm, and thus argues against the use of the food.

Spinach, which contains iron, also contains oxalic acid, which causes kidney stones. Iron can more safely be obtained from pills containing only iron, and no harmful substances.

Beef is another excellent source of iron, but contains potentially harmful fats and possible carcinogens. Beer decreases the production of LDLs, the harmful low-density lipoproteins which keep cholesterol in the body, while simultaneously increasing the production of HDLs, the beneficial high-density lipoproteins, which take cholesterol out of the body. Beer is also an appetite stimulant. But people who rely on beer alone to do the job risk acquiring other problems and not really solving the basic problem.

Some foods have remarkable healing or disease preventative qualities. For example, cranberries help prevent urinary tract infections, cheddar cheese fights tooth decay by inhibiting harmful bacteria, figs and prunes are excellent laxatives. Figs are rich in iron, and are a good source of calcium for osteoporosis sufferers. The pectin in apples is anti-diarrheal, and apples contain substances which interfere with the absorption by the body of dietary fats. The vitamin A in apricots helps lower the risk of certain cancers, and the apricot is rich in potassium—good news for people who lose potassium when they take diuretics.

Some doctors have advocated high doses of marine lipids—oils from fish such as salmon, shad, and mackerel—for treatment of cancer, arthritis, allergies, multiple-sclerosis, high triglyceride levels, and hypertension.

The list goes on and on. The distrust many doctors had of diet and health foods in the early 1900s has slowly given way to acceptance of nutrition as vital to curing disease and for preventive medicine. As research continues into the building blocks of common foods, more discoveries about their ability to prevent disease may be expected.

Junk Food: An American Oxymoron

We first taste sugar in mother's milk, put there by nature to induce us to drink the life-giving fluid. From that sweet beginning we plunge down into the dark-chocolate pit of guilt, fear, and punishment and into the maw of sin: obesity, diabetes, malnutrition . . . and bad teeth. In *Buddenbrooks,* Thomas Mann writes of a character who committed suicide by eating pastries. Had Mann been writing today, he could have added junk food to the scene of the crime.

The average American diet consists of 55 percent junk food, a type of so-called nourishment which did not even exist before World War II, when food shortages first created a demand for *ersatz* food. Recently junk food achieved the status of a mind-altering substance when an accused murderer told the court he couldn't help himself because he ate too many Twinkies.

The government informs us that each American runs the following quantities of junk food (or, as the industry euphemistically calls it, convenience, or fast food) through his or her system each year:

    50 pounds of cookies and cake

    63 dozen doughnuts

    100 pounds of refined sugar

    55 pounds of fat (and oil)

    300 containers of soda

    200 sticks of chewing gum

    20 gallons of ice cream

    5 pounds of potato chips

    18 pounds of candy

unknown quantities of popcorn, pretzels, and
a wide variety of snack foods (another euphemism).

If you think you can control junk food by reading labels, consider this puzzler on a two-ounce package of brand-name chips; a mixture of potatoes, oil, and salt. The oil in the chip may, or may not, be one of the following: sunflower oil, canola oil, corn oil, cottonseed oil, partially hydrogenated sunflower oil, partially hydrogenated canola oil, partially hydrogenated soy bean oil, peanut oil, or partially hydrogenated cottonseed oil. This little seventy-five-cent handful also contains 150 calories and ten grams of fat.

But at least you can understand those ingredients. Who but an expert can tell if the following ingredients are good or bad? All of them are in one or another junk food: Sodium propionate, Carrageenan, Dioctyl Sodium Sulfosuccinate, Gum Arabic, Guar Gum, Invert sugar, Invertase, Lecithin, Mannitol, Monoglycerides and Diglycerides, Polysorbate 60, Pro-

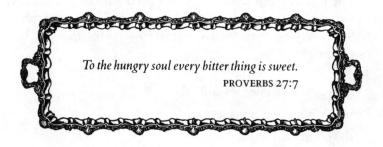

To the hungry soul every bitter thing is sweet.
PROVERBS 27:7

pyl Gallate, Propylene Glycol, Sodium Benzoate, Sodium Nitrite, Sodium Erythorbate, Sorbic Acid, Sorbitan Monostearate, Sorbitol, Tragacanth Gum, Monosodium Glutamate, Carboxymethyl Cellulose, Annato Color, Sulfite . . . and the list goes on.

If this list doesn't make your mouth water, the items on it will by ensuring bright, colorful products that taste good and keep for long periods without spoiling. Some of the products they appear in are actually nourishing and some are even good for you.

Junk food seems here to stay. To protect their health, concerned consumers must be constantly vigilant. We must become a nation of label-readers and question askers. Never has the ancient Roman warning "let the buyer beware" been more important.

Junk food does have one dubious advantage: modern bodies have so many preservatives in them that they are not decomposing as rapidly as they once did, according to undertakers. Let's just say that it doesn't seem enough to make it all worth it.

The German Navy and
the White Bread Torpedo

For eight months the *Kronprinz Wilhelm* sank ship after ship with impunity. The fastest cruiser in the German navy, she had racked up thirteen kills, commandeering cargoes and sending the hapless ships and their crews to the bottom. Then, one by one, the crew of the *Kronprinz* fell ill. Over one hundred had died, twenty percent of the crew, when on April 11, 1915, the ship finally docked in the then neutral United States.

Doctors who came aboard to investigate ruled out beri-beri, a disease caused by improper nutrition, because the hold of the ship was packed with tons of tinned meat, white flour, biscuits, sausages, smoked fish, coffee and tea, oleomargarine, cheeses; enough food to supply a small village for a year or more, all looted from their prey. So bountiful were the stolen cargoes that the *Kronprinz* had to deep-six the food they couldn't take, including two shiploads of whole wheat flour. Who needed it when there was so much refined white flour available?

The learned doctors pulled their beards, harrumphed, and gazed perplexedly at each other through their pince-nez spectacles. No one had a clue. No one, that is, except Al McCann, a loud-mouthed, muckraking journalist who worked as a reporter for the *New York Globe* and specialized in unmasking the unsavory practices of the food factories that dominated the markets of the United States. He had written two books attacking the medical profession for ignoring nutrition and diet and his name was poison in medical circles. So effective was he that his paper built a special laboratory for him to putter around in to research his stories.

Reporters had been barred from the ship, but McCann, sensing a scoop, posed as a doctor and sneaked aboard with a borrowed business card. He was immediately recognized and denounced but before anything could happen McCann announced he knew what ailed the crew and could cure them

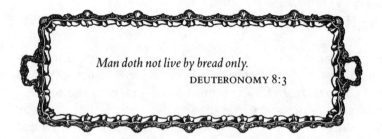

Man doth not live by bread only.
DEUTERONOMY 8:3

without drugs. He held forth so persuasively that the ship's doctor, officers, and assembled medical experts listened without interruption. When he finished he was invited to stay on board. McCann explained to the ship's doctor that despite the sumptuous food served lavishly to the crew, the processing of the food had removed the nutrients needed for survival. In the midst of plenty, the men were starving for nourishment and had contracted beri-beri and scurvy. The doctors did not suspect those illnesses because the men were obviously well-fed to excess. The reporter minced no words in his anger over the disposal of the cargoes of whole wheat, which could have saved the lives of the sailors.

McCann fed the crew water soaked overnight in unrefined wheat germ and bran, soup made by boiling unpeeled vegetables for two hours, glasses of the broth of boiled potato skins, and large glasses of fresh milk into which was mixed raw egg yolks. The men had to drink glasses of fresh orange and lemon juice and could eat as many fresh apples as they wanted.

The next day there were no new cases reported and within weeks the men were cured. Vitamins were not yet discovered and the laboratory link between them and good health was still years away. How did McCann know what to do? He was brilliant but he wasn't a doctor or scientist. Like many good newspapermen he operated on hunches and he did his homework.

One Man's Poison Is Another Man's Cure

The test of an optimist is to decide if the cup is half full or half empty. But what if the cup is poisoned and the one doing the testing is an ophthalmologist? Only an optimist like Dr. Alan Scott of the Smith-Kettlewell Eye Research Institute in San Francisco would find joy in that prospect.

The bane of the canning industry, botulism toxin is found in spoiled food and causes severe pain and often death. It is a muscle relaxant: the ultimate relaxant. The affected muscles relax so much they become paralyzed.

"What if . . . ?" the doctor wondered one day over a cup of coffee. He began experimenting with animals and was soon injecting minute quantities of the deadly poison into the eye muscles of patients with crossed eyes, wall eyes, and compulsive squints, symptoms of *strabismus,* a condition which leads to blindness if untreated. He also tried it out on *blepharospasm* victims, whose eyes twitch compulsively.

The resulting drug, *oculinum,* is now available commercially and goes by the nickname *botox.* A poison by any other name is still a poison and *botox* can cause death if an overdose is administered accidentally. There is no antidote.

Despite such cautions, the medical community is eager to experiment, and has used *botox* successfully for chronic torticollis, which distorts the neck, causes spasms of the vocal chord (which causes the victim to speak in whispers), spasms of the tongue and mouth, and other facial conditions that cause the jaw to lock shut or hang open, and writer's and musician's cramp, and has shown promise in curing certain types of constipation and bladder problems. It is even being considered as a treatment for stuttering.

The drug has limitations; there are side effects. Doctors who use it need special training. Next time you find a rusty, bulging food can in your pantry remember that the reverse of the old saw is equally true: one man's cure is another man's poison.

Pure Food Can Be Harmful

Sir Winston Churchill, Britain's redoubtable prime minister during World War II, drank daily, chain-smoked cigars, and was overweight. In addition to his prime-ministerial duties he was also a painter, author, historian, and amateur bricklayer. He died at age ninety-one with all his faculties intact. Everyone knows, or has heard of, someone robustly approaching their hundredth year, yet who daily violates all the rules of good health, especially those concerning eating and drinking.

"They are the exceptions that prove the rule," scoff the nutritionists, puffing away on their life-cycle machines. Most of us try to avoid eating and drinking to excess, or at the very least we scrutinize food labels for words of more than four syllables, a sure sign of lurking danger. No matter how hard we try it is impossible to avoid all food that is not healthy. Now it seems that even some foods long considered beyond reproach may also be dangerous to eat.

Sugar can ruin your teeth, give you a heart condition and, if you are diabetic, kill you. Honey and maple syrup are mainly sugar, and beets, carrots, and other fruits and vegetables are loaded with it.

Rhubarb and spinach contain oxalic acid which can produce kidney stones. Pure oxalic acid is a poison, used for bleaching fabrics and removing stains. It is present in spinach in minuscule amounts, not enough to harm anyone who eats it occasionally, unless they are prone to kidney stones. Nor is there enough iron or other nutrients present in spinach to justify eating it regularly and in quantity.

Nobody ever saw a rabbit wearing glasses, goes the joke that connects the rodent's love of carrots with good eyesight, a result of the vitamin A present in the root. Carrots are a good source of the vitamin, and it is helpful in certain types of retinal pigment loss connected with night-blindness.

But too much vitamin A from eating carrots, or drinking carrot juice to excess can be as dangerous as eating too much spinach. The body needs only a small amount of the vitamin and cannot discard it as readily as it does other vitamins. Carrots, egg yolks, mangoes, and sweet potatoes contain carotene, which gives them their orange color. The natural dye in carotene will color the human skin orange if ingested in large enough dosages, and in large quantities can cause jaundice. Licorice can raise your blood pressure and, as sold in this country, contains sugar. Cabbage can produce goiter under certain conditions.

Other veggies which have had the finger pointed at them are lima beans, almonds, nutmeg, avocados, and even the healthful onion.

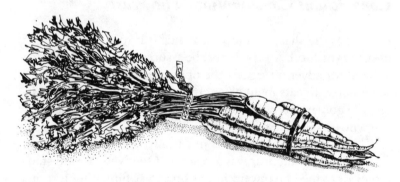

Frightened by such reports, a young man repaired to the English forests in 1977 to live off the land on nature's food, secure from the evils of additives and poisons. He was taken to a hospital a few days later near death. One of the pure foods he found in the woods turned out to be hemlock, the deadly poison that killed Socrates.

Three words uttered by one of the wisest of men, Aristotle, should be hung in every food store, restaurant, and kitchen:

"All things in moderation."

Chapter 5
Food and Culture

O woe, woe, man is only a dot:
Hell drags us off and that is the lot;
So let us live a little space,
At least while we can feed our face.

> Trimalchio's Lament, *The Satyricon*
> Petronius

Conspicuous Consumption: The Feast

Hunger is the sharpest sauce, it's said. But to really enjoy the pleasures of food, survival must be assured and enough money at hand for adventuring. At the opposite end of starvation are the diner who eats in an ostentatious manner to impress others, the gourmand who eats for sensual pleasure, and the glutton who eats to excess.

The appetite of Diamond Jim Brady, a legendary glutton from the Gay Nineties, was awesome. One New York restaurateur described Diamond Jim at breakfast funneling into his vast midriff a gallon of orange juice, three eggs, half a loaf of bread, a large steak with fried potatoes and onions, grits and bacon, muffins, and a stack of pancakes. Thus fortified, the financier worked through the morning, serenely awaiting lunch.

Typically, he got up to speed at the midday meal by eating three dozen oysters, two bowls of soup, a half-dozen crabs, seven or eight lobsters, a few portions of turtle meat, and a large steak with assorted vegetables. For dessert he polished off a platter of pastries and two pounds of chocolate candy. Brady sometimes ate four or five meals like that each day: breakfast, brunch, lunch, dinner, and a little something before retiring for the night. One restaurateur called him "the best twenty-five customers I ever had."

One dinner Brady particularly liked to recall was given by architect Stanford White. A huge pie was wheeled in, a dancer emerged, unclothed (but perhaps for a fragment of pie or two), and walked the length of the banquet table, stopping at Brady's seat and falling into his lap—or, one presumes, what she could find of it, given his vast girth. As she spoon-fed the millionaire, more dancers appeared, also *en dishabille,* and attended to the feeding needs of the other guests. The rest of the menu goes unrecorded.

The meal he most wanted to forget took place at Luchow's in New York. His dinner guest was Lillian Russell, the most famous actress in America and the toast of four continents. Naturally, the couple drew a certain amount of attention. At a certain point in the meal, Brady took out a leather case. The other customers watched fascinated as he opened it. Inside was one million dollars in cash. Removing his napkin from around his neck, Brady carefully placed it on the floor and knelt on it. He then proposed to her with the romantic words, "This is all yours if you'll marry me." As the other diners strained to hear, Russell cast a careless look at the money and called the waiter over. "I'd like some more Beluga caviar," she said.

Diamond Jim was a gastronomic showman who reflected the times—an era of pompous vulgarity. His interests turned from gem stones to kidney stones five years before his death in 1917, when he endowed the James Buchanan Brady Urological Institute at Johns Hopkins. When he died, his autopsy revealed a stomach six times that of a normal person.

Delmonico's restaurant in New York, another of Diamond Jim's favored hangouts, featured exotic foods such as ptarmigan (grouse), truffled pig's feet, bear and deer steak, green turtles, and those staples of the culinary elite: French champagne and beluga caviar.

Another eager eater was Louis XIV of France, whose stomach was found to be twice the size of a normal stomach upon his death. At a typical meal Louis would eat four bowls of soup for starters, followed by a couple of pheasants or a partridge, a large salad, several slices of ham or other meat, mutton, hard-boiled eggs, several pastries and some fruit. A grisly postscript to the death of the monarch occurred when grave robbers stole Louis's heart away during the French Revolution. The heart eventually found its way to England where it was purchased by The Very Reverend William Buckland, Dean of Westminster, who ate it.

Belshazzar, the last king of Babylon, threw a feast the unexpected highlight of which was handwriting which appeared magically on the wall, and whose message, *Mene, mene, tekel upharsin,* "You have been weighed in the scales and found wanting," was ignored. Like many historical feasts, it was a way of snapping collective fingers in the face of doom. Belshazzar was subsequently defeated and killed by Cyrus.

Feasting on the knife's edge has always fascinated; metaphorists are fond of using the merrymaking aboard the Titanic to illustrate the point. Late eighteenth-century French aristocracy munched truffles as revolution brewed. In the second decade of this century, the Romanov's featured champagne, caviar, and French conversation at their feasts while the masses rioted outside the palace walls.

The Egyptians were not noted for decadent feasts, but the nobility and priests ate well. There were dozens of different kinds of bread and cakes made with barley, honey, eggs, and milk. A variety of fish and fowl was available and considerable time was spent hunting wild animals. The Egyptians had cheese, beef, fresh berries, and many different kinds of vegetables, often gathered in the wild.

However, when the Roman Empire took control of the known world, so much money came to them from their conquests that they had plenty to party with. Perhaps the most famous (or infamous) food-fest in history was Trimalchio's Banquet which took place in the first century A.D. in Rome and was recorded by Petronius in *The Satyricon.* Petronius, dubbed "the judge of elegance" by Tacitus, was director of entertainment in Nero's court and an expert on staging parties where money was no object. This feast, perhaps, exceeded even his flair for opulence.

The guests' hands, so his account tells us, were rinsed with iced water and their toenails were clipped by servants singing loudly and off-key, apparently to everyone's great amusement. Appetizers appeared, starting with a bronze ass loaded with black and white olives. Iron contraptions supported cooked dormice drizzled in honey and sesame seeds. Steaming sausages were served on a silver grill with plums and pomegranate seeds underneath to simulate hot coals.

The next course arrived with an orchestral fanfare: a large tray with a wooden hen sitting on a nest of pastry eggs. Servants distributed them to the diners, each of whom sat at individual tables. Inside each egg was a cooked bird, a figpecker, afloat in peppered egg yolk.

Mead was served, followed by one-hundred-year-old bottled wine. During the evening the host kept up a running commentary on how much money he had, how much property and slaves he owned, how superior he, a freed slave, was to the free-born Romans present, and how beautiful his wife was.

Trimalchio recited a poem he wrote (quoted at the beginning of this chapter), and the next course arrived: a large tray with signs of the zodiac around the edge and symbolic dishes over each sign. The food was not appealing but, as the guests prepared to politely begin eating anyway, the servants whisked away the top of the tray, revealing the true course below. Under the false top were fowls, pigs udders, and a hare with wings made to look like a flying horse, all of which were set among statues of satyrs, each holding a bottle of sauce that flowed into a channel in which cooked fish seemed to swim. A carver cut the meat in rhythm to the orchestra's music.

As Trimalchio lectured his audience about the signs of the zodiac, the doors suddenly opened and servants entered with hunting gear, followed by a pack of hunting dogs who bounded around the room. In the midst of the commotion more servants entered, bearing a huge roasted boar wearing a hat and with baskets of Syrian and Egyptian dates dangling from his tusks.

As everyone gasped, a servant costumed as a hunter slashed the boar open. A flock of live thrushes flew out and around the room, where they were caught by servants and distributed to the guests as gifts. Cakes made to look like piglets were also distributed to take home.

Next, three live pigs were trotted into the room and the guests asked to choose which they wanted. This done, the pigs trotted back to the kitchen. Soon, an enormous roasted pig was wheeled out. Trimalchio accused the slave of failing to gut it and ordered him stripped and flayed. The man begged for mercy. The merciful Trimalchio handed him a knife and told him to atone for his error by gutting the pig right then and there. As the slave slashed away, cooked sausages and blood puddings spilled from inside it—the guests had been fooled again!

Trimalchio's accountant then regaled the crowd with a report on Trimalchio's financial affairs; acrobats entertained as the guests sipped wine. Trimalchio generously gave a slave boy his freedom and the guests listened to their host's philosophical ramblings as they drew chits from a bowl for humorous gifts.

Arguments broke out among the guests, many of whom were by now quite drunk. Costumed actors recited verses from Homer. The next course arrived: an entire calf boiled whole and served wearing a helmet. The two-hundred-pound serving tray was put down and the calf was carved dramatically by one of the actors.

The ceiling of the room shook, panels opened, and a hoop descended into the room, on which were hung alabaster jars of toilet cream and gold crowns: more gifts for Trimalchio's lucky guests.

An enormous tray of cakes was placed on the serving table.

In the center of the tray was a pastry penis, surrounded at its base by apple and grape testicles. As the delighted guests reached for the sweets, a cloud of saffron puffed in their faces.

The besotted guests became pious and blessed their emperor. Statues of several gods were brought out, including a gold statue of Trimalchio which the guests kissed devoutly. A lamp broke and hot oil spilled on some guests. A fight broke out among pet dogs, more guests arrived, and a fracas was staged by two servants carrying water jugs. The jugs broke in the mock battle and oysters and scallops poured out. They were gathered up and served to the diners. Several more such inventive courses were served.

Trimalchio argued with his wife and flung his glass in her face, reducing her to tears. Other guests wandered about, some falling into the pool. By this time it was the next day; the servants had changed shifts but the feasting continued.

Trimalchio lay down and asked the guests to pretend they were at his funeral and say what they would say of him at that time. The orchestra played a dirge so loudly the fire department thought the alarm had been sounded and broke into the house with axes and water. During the commotion Petronius, who by now was thoroughly disgusted, slipped out and went home to write his report.

Roman decadence is well-publicized; what isn't generally known is that the Romans operated what today would be considered a vast welfare state, not because they were particularly concerned with humanitarian causes: it was a way to ensure a peaceful population. It was cheaper, they reasoned, to give away grain than to police the population to suppress food riots and other rebellions. The army would be better employed extending and safeguarding the far-flung empire.

When Rome was young, the citizens ate frugally. A typical meal consisted of black bread, thick soup, cooked vegetables and fruit, and perhaps a bit of poultry, meat, or fish. Slaves ate even more sparingly. By the second century B.C. there were such food shortages that the tribune, Gaius Gracchus, began subsidizing grain for the citizenry. Fifty years later free grain was available and the practice then became the rule for hundreds of years. By the time Trimalchio had his little party, up to one-third of the population of Rome got free grain and other foods.

The era of great Roman feasts lasted from about the first century before Christ to approximately A.D. 300, when the empire began to unravel. The feasts were confined to the upper classes: the government, military rulers, and rich businessmen. Average Romans ate well, but their nutrition was not significantly improved, nor was the variety of their cuisine expanded much by the wealth of the empire.

Control of food was power; to the Romans it meant showing off at table. Then, as now, a free meal guaranteed a captive audience looking for diversion and gossip. As the account of Trimalchio's banquet reveals, the Romans made up in novelty what they lacked in culinary technique. The most successful feasts were those with the most spectacular effects, the most slaves, the most presents for the guests, and the greatest variety of foods presented in unusual ways: camel heels, roasted peacocks with the feathers stuck back on, ostriches, cranes, flamingos, storks, and pheasant by the hundreds. Bird brains and tongues were as desirable as caviar today, and just as expensive.

Roman extravagance (in quantity, if not in quality) was revived briefly by the Church toward the end of the Middle Ages. When the Archbishop of York was enthroned in 1467, the cooks ordered three hundred tons of ale, one hundred tons of wine, one hundred oxen for roasting, three hundred pigs, three hundred calves, four hundred swans, and a thousand sheep. In 1542 the Archbishop of Canterbury decreed that his dinner should be limited to not more than six meat courses, and four entrees to follow.

The poor in Medieval times (as always) ate what they could, but for the nobility, the feast was an entertainment and often a political statement, a series of encounters during which the shrewd guest from another kingdom assessed the military strength of his hosts by the bounty of their board. In the councils that followed the return of the guest to his kingdom, descriptions of the feasts were weighed with as much gravity as any other factor.

The magnificence and variety of Medieval banquets was not to impress resident vassals with their prince's wealth so much as to induce the conclusion that a prince who could offer such a magnificent feast was too strong to be meddled with.

So important was the idea of wealth expressed through food that the process of *endoring* was developed: Food presented in a manner to suggest gold. Any method to make a dish appear golden—using dyes such as saffron, glazes, even putting gold foil on food—was desirable. Egg yolks were used in enormous quantities for this purpose. In 1387, the larder of King Richard II included 132,000 eggs for his household for one year.

Feasting promoted good public relations for the prince's subjects as well. Word of sumptuous feasts quickly got around, bringing loyalty and pride and the feeling that their prince was strong and able to protect them (as well as softening rebellious thoughts).

During the Middle Ages it was common practice for the lord of the castle to dine in a large hall at his special table, and to have many lower tables at which dined his vassals and some of the local poor. If the courses prepared for the lord smelled good, he would often order portions distributed to the lower tables. He satisfied himself that he was taking good care of his charges and they, in turn, dined in the same room with their lord, eating the same food, and seeing his witnessing of this. It all made for loyalty and good feeling.

This began to change around the middle of the fourteenth century when the lord and lady, his guests, and his retinue dined in a separate room. The custom of the Middle Ages of everyone dining in one large hall gave way to privacy and the separation of classes which reached its height in the Victorian

era. It also separated the cuisine of the master from that of the servant, allowing for the development of *haute cuisine.*

Medieval feasts suggest people with huge appetites consuming unbelievable quantities of food. There were a few gluttons in those days of course, and what records exist of food habits indicate that the idea "more is better" was the order of the day, but actually the lords and ladies picked and chose from among their dinner items with care and relative moderation. It was not so much the quantity as the variety of food, the ability of the host to scour the kingdom and the world for delicacies to present at the feast that was important; it was a demonstration of the lord's ability to command. The feast was a propaganda ritual.

Cooks outdid themselves to amuse and astonish their lords. The Medieval fascination with fantastic animals was indulged in the kitchen. The front of a chicken would be sewn to the back of a pig and presented on a platter. Jelly was dyed and textured to form coats of arms, and so were pastries. Birds, animals, and even people popped out of fake pies to the delight of guests. Entire tableaux were made of pastry, bread, and lard, then painted and decorated with edible greens and fruits.

The theme dinner was an invention of the Medieval chamberlains. A dinner would have a nautical theme, or a Biblical theme, to commemorate a special event. Craftsmen made platters in the shape of ships, or whatever the theme was, and the chef would oblige with themed dishes.

Medieval food was a tool of power; in modern times it has again become a sensual and esthetic indulgence for those who can afford the cost.

Red Meat

Mao Tse Tung vowed every family in China would one day own a pig. Apparently, there wasn't much political mileage to be had from cattle, sheep, or goats. Although China can support these animals, the Chinese show little enthusiasm for their meat, milk, or cheese. Whether insufficient lactase (necessary to digest lactose in milk) in their systems caused the Chinese to avoid milk and milk products, or whether the absence of milk-producing animals in their agricultural realm caused their bodies to eventually cease producing lactase has been disputed by biologists.

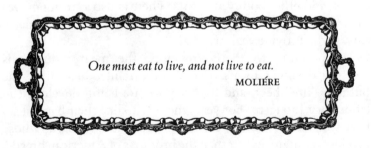

One must eat to live, and not live to eat.
MOLIÉRE

Nor can these staples (except beef) be found in Chinese restaurants. They may represent a cultural bias from the days when China's traditional enemies were the conquering nomadic tribesmen who pillaged the countryside with their hated herds mooing, baaing, and bleating behind them.

Observant Jews won't eat pork. The proscription goes back to Moses' proclamation, "And the swine shall be unclean to you." In biblical days the wandering Jews were shepherds. Pigs can't be herded; they require a stationary existence. Farmers (pig-raisers) were often the nomadic Jews' traditional enemies.

Cleanliness, next only to godliness for the Jews, became such a preoccupation that swine may have been avoided simply because they were filthy. The connection between pork and illness may have been intuited by them (anthropologists point out sniffily that the trichinosis worm was only identified in 1835); butchering a pig in biblical days often revealed worms and other large, visible parasites, enough evidence for the Jews.

In the vastness of the early American west, the enmity between shepherds and farmers became a conflict between the range and the grange. Bloody shootouts involving hired thugs like Billy the Kid were common. Range wars were brief and localized and left few scars on the national psyche (though providing seemingly limitless plots for movie westerns).

In 1987 the per capita consumption of red meat in the United States was 144 pounds. Americans are lovers of meat, although this is changing in light of links between meat and cancer, and other bodily ailments. There is also a strong movement under way to curtail the way meat animals, particularly calves who provide veal, are treated.

Responding to these pressures, the meat industry is creating designer meats. Beefalo, the reintroduction of the buffalo, "lite" beef, and lighter pork are being developed in laboratory and farm. For years those who like their bacon lean have sought the canned bacon of Poland and Denmark, whose products contain less fat than the products of American breeds, that does not shrink to annoyingly minuscule proportions in the pan as the fat burns off. Scientists at the University of Illinois in Urbana have produced pigs with fewer saturated fats by feeding them a diet high in polyunsaturated fats. Normally, pigs raised in the corn belt are fed a combination of corn and soybean meal, from which the beneficial polyunsaturated soy-bean oil has been removed—along with many vitamins and minerals. Pigs in the study ate whole soybeans for three to six weeks before they were slaughtered. Pigs on the soybean diet produced bacon (and the leaner cuts as well) with 8 percent less saturated fats than those not on the diet. The amount of fat didn't change, only the ratio of saturated fats to unsaturated fats.

In any event, pigs today are less fat-producing than pigs nine years ago. Comparative tests at the University of Wisconsin at Madison found that a three ounce portion of cooked lean pork averaged 31 percent less fat, 10 percent less cholesterol, and 17 percent less calories than those tested a decade earlier. They attribute this to changes in breeding and feeding regimens and better trimming by butchers.

The Japanese adore beef, but cannot get enough because their country is too small for large-scale cattle raising. An exception are the Wadakin and Matsuzuka cows of Kobe, who live the good life; they drink beer, are massaged three times a day to keep their meat tender, and are sung to, making them feel serene. Kobe beef is world-famous, although chances of finding any outside Japan are almost nil. A few restaurants in the United States import the rare commodity, charging the curious one-hundred dollars for a sixteen-ounce, one-inch thick steak.

Burial at Sea

There are several misconceptions about sea food which should be buried.

Soft-shelled crabs are a special breed of crab. Their shell, so goes the assumption, for some counter-evolutionary reason, is soft. The soft-shell crab is really the blue crab, named for the distinctive bright blue color of its shell, caught after it molts its old shell and before the new, soft shell has a chance to harden.

Shrimp must be deveined before eating. As our garbage reaches to the sky, we fastidious Americans concern ourselves with hygienic trivia that 98 percent of the rest of the world ignores. Yet each day we ingest insect eggs, vermin parts, rat droppings, dirt, and other foreign matter in prepared breads, cookies, flour, candy, and other products. Chocolate manufacturers, for example, are allowed by law to have up to 4 percent cockroach parts in their products. Because we can't see it, it doesn't bother us. The black vein running down the back of a shrimp is the waste of the shrimp's digestive process. It is tasteless and harmless but has the same effect on finicky diners as seeing dirty fingernails.

Scallops are fish. Actually, scallops are mollusks, as are clams, oysters, and mussels. This castanet of the sea moves around by snapping its shell, propelling itself by ejecting a jetstream of escaping water. What we eat is the highly developed muscle, a tasty, tender morsel. So beautiful is the design of its fluted shell that it was once a badge for religious pilgrims and is the trademark of a famous oil company. Some unscrupulous restaurants substitute nuggets of cheaper fish for the more expensive scallops.

There is something in a lobster that will kill you if you eat it. The only thing inedible in the lobster (besides the shell) is the stomach, located behind the eyes, and the long black vein attached to it. These are not poisonous, merely inedible. Anyhow, most Americans ignore this area and go for the luscious meat in the tail and claws. The bilious-looking yellow-green liver is delicious and a gourmet delight.

Oysters may only be eaten in a month with an r in the name. Perhaps before modern refrigeration the risk of getting poisoned from spoiled oysters was real, especially in the warm *r*-less months from May through August. That's also when oysters breed, and the real reason for the proscription. To ensure a good oyster crop the beds are left undisturbed in these months, sometimes by state law. Aficionados claim that oysters taken during breeding season are tasteless. Fresh oysters are available year-around in most major metropolitan cities, so the point has become moot in recent years.

Mother Corn

The French disdain for corn is shared by many Europeans who consider the vegetable Americans love fit only for hog feed. Nor is it vegetable xenophobia because the French (and other Europeans) readily accepted other foods from the New World.

Christopher Columbus brought back maize from his explorations. The new crop could be grown anywhere as a cheap substitute for wheat. The poor began to plant it and some, to live off it. A plague soon spread over Europe characterized by fissures in the skin, running sores, insanity and death. It was called *pel agre,* the rough skin disease, shortened to *pellagra,* and struck those living on a diet of corn (maize) and little else.

Yet millions of people in the western hemisphere ate corn for millennia with no ill effects; the difference was they balanced their diets with other foods. Nonetheless, at the turn of the century pellagra was a major disease in the United States because of widespread poverty and ignorance of proper nutrition. In 1930, in the depths of the Depression, there were 250,000 cases of pellagra and over 7,000 deaths. Hospitals and insane asylums filled with victims.

After heroic medical detective work the puzzle of pellagra was solved. Corn does not contain enough tryptophan, an amino acid the body turns into vitamin B (niacin). Unless other foods are eaten which contain tryptophan, pellagra results.

Doctor Joseph Goldberger, who came to the United States from Austria as a child, did much of the research that led to the eradication of pellagra, and discovered the nature of and remedy for the disease. Dr. Goldberger contracted yellow fever, diphtheria, typhus, and dengue fever in the course of his distinguished and heroic career in medical research. He spent over a decade (1913 to 1925) in the search for a cure for pellagra and was nominated (unsuccessfully) five times for the Nobel Prize in medicine. The medical profession, convinced that the cure for pellagra would be found in medicine and not nutrition, denied him the honors he so richly deserved. Dying of cancer, he learned of the Nobel committee decision against him and asked that a letter be sent telling the committee that no prize on earth was worth more than the love and honor of his colleagues.

Corn is grown in such quantities and has so many functions in our society that the average person eats corn in some form every day without realizing it. Almost everything in the store, except fresh fish, has been touched in some way by corn. All meat contains corn, fed to livestock and poultry to make them fat and healthy. Their milk and eggs were produced with the nutrients in the corn and cornstalks they ate. Corn starch is coated on the surface of frozen meat and fish to prevent freezer drying, and many foods and soft drinks are colored appealingly with corn dyes.

Corn oil is an important ingredient in hundreds of foods. Corn is used to make the containers that food is sold in and is an ingredient in soap, insecticides, mayonnaise, and prepared salad dressings. Even monosodium glutamate, the favorite mystery seasoning of Chinese restaurants, is made with corn protein. Most candy contains corn syrup, as does ketchup, ice cream, condensed milk, and many beers and hard liquors.

Corn starch is in baby food, packaged yeast, vinegar, pickles and jams, and is an additive in sugar and salt to make them easier to pour. It is an important ingredient in dehydrated foods such as powdered milk and potatoes, and is found in toothpaste, headache pills, dog food, matches, cosmetics, detergents and charcoal briquettes. Leathers and textiles are treated with corn. Corn helps adhesives to stick and prevents hard candies from sticking to each other. Materials used to build houses, roads, and cars contain corn, and it is an important component in the manufacture of furniture.

The durability of corn is legendary. Kernels stored for ten years will germinate. In one instance, archaeologists who found thousand-year-old corn in a ruin were amazed to see one of the pack donkeys eat some of it. Popcorn one thousand years old was successfully popped and tasted good, according to reports. Corn plants are so vigorous they will grow up to four and a half inches per day. Farmers claim they can actually hear corn growing in the field as the leaves unfurl and stretch open, creaking and crackling in their rows. And yet the vigor of the corn plant, its very existence, depends on mankind, for the corn plant would not exist without cultivation. There are so many kernels on one cob that, if they fell off the cob in one place, the seedlings would choke each other and all would die.

Not counting the awesome quantities of popcorn consumed in movie theaters around the country, the average American eats three pounds of corn, or corn products, or meats containing corn, every day. And this represents only one tenth of total corn production.

Excavations in Mexico City uncovered corn pollen dated

to eighty thousand years ago, in a period between ice ages. The mystery of how corn was cultivated and brought to its present form, like the origin of fire, may never be known. Corn is so ubiquitous in western society it has become a euphemism for something trite. It sounds corny, but America would be a different and poorer country today without corn, "our mother," as the Indians called it.

Bread and Love, Italian-Style

The passionate Italians are nowhere more passionate than when it comes to baking bread and pastry. Nuns in Sicilian convents knead almond dough into the shape of breasts, symbolizing the sliced-off breasts of St. Agatha. The sweet treats are prized confections at parties, where they compete with rum babas shaped like phalluses. In Medieval Italy, couples copulated in the wheat fields at planting time to ensure a fruitful harvest. Today the symbolism lingers in a bread called *coppiette,* baked in forms suggestive of copulation. Italians are in love with their breads and pastries. What other country has a dial-a-dough number where one can call from any part of Italy and get a recipe for a regional bread, with a different message every day?

What other country would set up a society to safeguard the purity of the native language and name it after bread? The *Accademia della Crusca* (bran) has the responsibility of sifting the linguistic wheat from the chaff. Their symbol is a flour-sifter.

Watch an Italian as he grabs a wheel of bread in the crook of his arm, gazes at it the way Isaac Stern looks at his violin before he plays it, and slices it with a huge knife aimed at his heart. A loaf of bread is an extension of the church wafer, a metaphor for the flesh of Jesus. Before closing the oven, the baker crosses himself, to bless the bread. Leave a knife in a loaf and you have put a knife into the heart of Jesus; be prepared for bad luck. Should you place a loaf back on the table upside down, you are again in big trouble. Drop some on the floor and it must be picked up, cleaned off, and eaten, or more bad luck will come. Purgatory is the punishment for wasting bread. Nobody plays games with bread in Italy.

Before Rome was an empire, inhabitants of the Italian boot customarily buried the wife with the husband, even if it was not her time to die. As Italy became more civilized, a wife was permitted to live, but had to cut her braided hair off and bury it with her husband as a symbol of devotion. In time, even that practice was abandoned when someone invented braided bread as an acceptable substitute. It was not buried in the coffin, but given to the local poor.

Italians eat more bread per capita, a half-pound per day on average, than any other people in Europe. Four-and-a-half billion pounds of bread are consumed each year by the fifty-seven million people who live there. Bread is served at every meal, in every restaurant. Consumers in Italy are so involved with bread that bakeries not only show the price of each bread, but list the ingredients on the sign.

The Italian language is rich with bread metaphors and proverbs. If you know the difference between a loaf of bread and a rock, you are a savvy person, not easily fooled. If you are "good as bread," *e buono come il pane,* you can be trusted. If it's "not bread for your teeth," *non e pane per i tuoi denti,* you are not up to the task and should look for a lesser challenge. Even the weather reminds Italians of their favorite food. *Sotto la neve e pane,* loosely translated, means "when it snows, the wheat grows better." When someone has temporarily gotten the upper hand over an Italian, revenge is promised with the saying, *pan tosto per te sta riposto,* "Don't worry, stale bread is in store for you." The words are accompanied by one of several hand gestures which are not translatable.

Every part of Italy, every region, every city and village, has a bread or pastry of its own. There are breads for special occasions and holidays. The Easter bread has eggs baked inside, an ancient symbol of the resurrection. The *pannetone* bread of Christmas is sweet, like the Christ child, and a traditional gift of the season. There's a special bread for shepherds, another one for sailors. Columbus took *biscotti* (twice-baked bread) on his long voyage, as did Marco Polo.

There is a special bread for the dead, and a bone-shaped cookie, *ossa di morte,* eaten in honor of the dead on All Souls Day. In Calabria there is a bread baked only when a local leaves town on a journey. It is stamped with an image of the Madonna and blessed by the priest.

The fascination with bread goes back to the proud days of ancient Rome. So important was bread to the Romans that a special goddess of the ovens, Fornax, was honored each year by placing flowers over all ovens. In 25 B.C. there were over three hundred bakeries in Rome. In A.D. 100 a school for bakers was founded by Trajan. Bakers, usually freed slaves, were not permitted to change their vocations. Their sons had to follow in the father's floury footsteps; once a baker, always a baker.

In the 1950s and 1960s, huge factories went up all over Italy, baking bread on a mechanized assembly-line with no character. The beloved breadsticks of Italy came out like tubes, each exactly like the next, with a dry, tasteless consistency. The breads were rectangular bricks, with no variation in the texture, and tasted like they were made in a factory by robots, and not in the turmoil of a small Italian bakery, where the perspiring baker puts his creative soul into each loaf, and fashions the design on the outside as lovingly as he blends the wholesome ingredients in the loaf.

For a while it looked as if Italy would go the way of the United States, a loaf of tasteless white bread on each table. But it was only a temporary setback. Organizations were formed to preserve the breads of the past, schools taught the old recipes, and lecturers touted the glories of fresh bread. Today, the old breads are back, and exciting new breads are being invented that will some day become traditional.

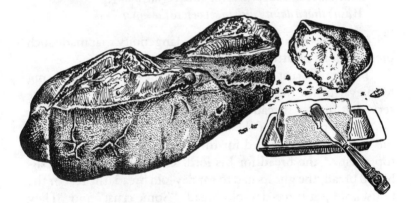

Tradition! Tradition!

Raising the pinkie finger to indicate delicacy comes from Medieval times when people ate with their fingers. Certain fingers were reserved for various foods. To keep them clean, the unused fingers were raised out of the way while the appropriate fingers did their jobs. The upper classes washed their hands between courses and after the meal. If rings were worn, they were placed on the pinkie finger, which was raised to keep them clean while eating. Wearing a ring on the pinkie survives in parts of Europe as a sign of class.

A tradition that had a brief revival in the 1920s was that of having something (or someone) emerge from a cake. During Medieval times, dummy pie shells were filled with live birds or frogs just before serving, and then, when the pie was cut, released to fly around the room, to the delight of the guests. Some innovative chamberlains would have a dwarf emerge and walk down the length of the table, reciting poetry, sketching the guests, or doing tricks. Indeed, this type of spectacle is the origin of the familiar nursery song:

> *"Four-and-twenty blackbirds, baked in a pie,*
> *When the pie was opened, the birds began to sing,*
> *Wasn't that a dainty dish to set before the king?"*

It was the element of surprise and ingenuity that made such presentations a feature of Medieval banquets.

The upper crust is a euphemism for the upper class. During Medieval times the master of the castle was the first to be served at dinner. Bread baked that day was presented by the *pantler*, the guardian of the bread. Using a special knife called the *mensal knife*, reserved for this purpose, the *pantler* cut the top crust of the bread for his lord. Only the lord had fresh-baked bread, the guests had to eat day-old bread, the rest of the household got three-day-old bread. "Some crust" and "They have a lot of crust," scornful epithets for those with pretensions to be more important than they actually are, come from the same source.

Caveat Emptor

The butcher with his thumb on the scale has a long and ignoble history. *Caveat emptor!* "Let the buyer beware," said the worldly Romans, acknowledging consumer-directed larceny as part of the human condition. In Medieval times, merchant duplicity resulted in dozens of laws to protect the consumer, (aptly called a subject in those days).

Bread was imprinted with the baker's seal so an offending loaf could be traced. Short-weighting was the most common offense; some bakers wrapped rancid dough in a coating of fresh dough before baking, others inserted an iron bar in a loaf to make a load of loaves weigh more. Bakers used molding boards to form the dough into a loaf before the customer's eyes and baked it to order. They were banned in London after nine bakers were caught with confederates hidden underneath the molding board and scooping dough from the already weighed loaves through a hole in the board, secretly unplugged from beneath.

The pillory or the hurdle was the punishment for errant bakers. Those that were *hurdled* were tied to a sled with their dishonest loaves hung around their necks and hauled around town to the jeers of onlookers. Three-time offenders were barred from their trade.

Dishonest piemen had a field day. The meat pie, or *pastie,* was an early version of take-out food, a complete meal in a pie. Pie-sellers often sold beef pies as venison, baked fish that was spoiled and heavily spiced to conceal the deficiency, or added offal, the unwanted cuts of meat, to pies.

Wines were routinely adulterated and watered until standards finally were imposed. In London, a member of a party drinking at a tavern had the right to demand to see the wine cellar, which was unbarred for the purpose. Refusal by the taverner could result in severe penalties, including, at times, prison. A wine-seller who diluted good wine with spoiled sometimes was forced to drink his wine, had the remainder poured over his head, and then sobered up in the pillory. The seals, ribbons, branded corks, and other traditional decorations on today's wine bottles are relics of Medieval efforts to safeguard the public against tampered wine.

Food additives are ambiguous. The phrase is benign, and

implies that the additive will make the substance it is added to better, more nutritious, longer-lasting. That is often the case, or at least the intent of those doing the adding-to. Unfortunately, sometimes the additives contain hidden dangers that can cause trouble later. Some additives are put into food for the cynical reason that they will produce a better bottom line by extending shelf-life, enhancing color to make the product more appealing, and so on. When an additive is added for reasons other than the purest of motives, and when its presence is not revealed openly to the purchaser, it becomes an adulterant, a word with evil overtones and a long, scurrilous history.

In 1884 a study of the food of the London poor revealed that milk often came from diseased cows and was routinely watered; the meat was the waste of the slaughterhouses, and often rotten as well. Used tea leaves were purchased from hotels, adulterated with lead to bring back the color of fresh tea, and sugar was added for the missing flavor. The resulting mess was further extended by adding sweepings from the floor. Stale flour had alum added to it to make it whiter, and ammonium and magnesium carbonate to mask the flavor of old flour.

The only thing sold to the poor unadulterated was gin.

Silver Lining in a Food Shortage

The entire country of Denmark went on a diet during World War I, when food was running out and the specter of starvation loomed. Instead of appointing a politician to solve the problem, the wise Danes appointed a nutritionist and gave him sweeping powers. For a while the Danes ate an abundance of meat because Dr. Mikkel Hindhede, the new food advisor to the government, ordered thousands of pigs and cows killed in order to save the grains fed to them as food and make them available directly to the population. He also ordered liquor factories closed and beer breweries cut to 50 percent capacity for the same reason.

With the supply of barley, malt, and other grains saved as a result of these actions, and the curtailment of white bread manufacturing, the Danes were forced to eat dark brown bread made of rye, whole wheat bran, and barley. They had plenty of potatoes, and oatmeal porridge, root vegetables and green vegetables, and some milk, eggs, fruit and cheese. There was almost no meat available and no hard liquor.

They avoided starvation and had an unexpected bonus. The death rate fell to the lowest recorded not only in Denmark, but in any other European country. The healthy diet had saved 6,300 from death by overeating and improper diet.

What's for Breakfast?

The dishes listed on the menus of ethnic restaurants or served to foreigners in the host country are often show-pieces, specialties developed over the centuries which the restaurateurs and chefs proudly offer as typical of their country's cuisine.

Typical of what? The food served in Cantonese Chinese restaurants was what Chinese peasants brought with them when they came to this country a century-and-a-half ago to work in the mines and on the railroads. The food eaten by the mandarins and emperors, and food from other parts of China, are very different. Visitors to urban Mexico are surprised at the sophistication of menus in fine restaurants, and the variety of cuisines within that country. The tacos and beans of state-side Mexican restaurants are there, but they are the fare of the campesinos, the food eaten by immigrants who came to the states and opened "Mexican" restaurants.

Go into a Brazilian, Chilean, or Argentinean restaurant in the United States and you will likely be eating food typical of the middle and upper economic classes of those countries. Those immigrants had money, were usually well-educated, and moved here because they could afford to. The poor of those countries cannot make such expensive and complicated moves as readily as the poor of nearby or bordering countries.

If any meal in a country can be called typical it is probably breakfast, a meal without pretensions in most countries, eaten to start the day, without regard to social niceties and complex ingredients. Here are some breakfasts typical of some foreign countries. They may not be eaten exactly as described, nor by all the population in every part of the country and in every economic bracket, but chances are good that in each case, a majority of the population enjoys a breakfast every morning similar to those listed.

FRANCE

A just-baked croissant or baguette with butter, and a large cup of steaming *café au lait* in which to dip it.

ENGLAND

Salty bacon and sausage with an egg, toast, and dark, tangy orange marmalade. Danish pastry. Coffee.

SCOTLAND

Oatmeal, kippers, bread, and oatcakes. Marmalade.

Northern Ireland

Bacon and eggs, fried cabbage, and potato mush.

United States

Orange juice, bacon and eggs, hash-brown potatoes, waffle with syrup; or, corn flakes with milk, half a grapefruit. Several cups of coffee.

China

Dim Sum—a selection of snacks: buns stuffed with spiced meat, steamed dumplings, duck, spiced rice, sausages, lots of tea.

South China

Rice porridge (jook) with slivers of fish, frog, or preserved egg. Hot soybean milk with onions.

Egypt

Felafel: mashed garbanzo beans, garlic and green onions fried in a patty and served in a pita (pocket bread).

Israel

A selection of cheeses, smoked and pickled fish, scrambled eggs, rolls and bread, yogurt, olives, tomatoes, cucumbers, pastry.

Mexico

Chilaquiles: tortillas with hot and spicy meat and cheese.

Philippines

Garlic-fried rice, dried fish.

VIETNAM
Rice noodle soup and bean sprouts.

JAPAN
Steaming rice porridge with vegetables and spicy pickles.

SPAIN
A cup of coffee.

PORTUGAL
Fresh bread slathered with butter. Coffee.

Are You Sure You Want to Eat That?

A voyage into the history of food soon leads to unpleasant discoveries. Food that is strange, funny, or horrifying to Americans—worms, bugs, snakes, or people who eat each other—do not represent weirdness or insanity but are almost always based on some logical historical development that led to the practice.

More often, the unpleasantness is subtler: the skin that forms on the surface of heated milk, the sliminess of okra or oysters trigger revulsions and physical reactions that are very real despite their mysterious origins.

Often the reason for the food being eaten no longer exists, yet the food lingers on in the national cuisine. A recent report on Fiji states that the island country could become self-sufficient in food production if the inhabitants would only eat taro, which grows readily in the South Pacific. But the residents, many descended from Asian and Indian immigrants, prefer rice, imported at enormous expense. Cultural habits die hard.

EELS

The American disgust for eels is exceeded only by our horror of snakes. Most of the world's people eat eels. The Roman emperor Heliogabulus raised conger eels for the table and fed them live slave meat in the belief it made them tastier. Conger eels are popular in Chile, where they are served with a meuniere sauce. Italians eat roasted eel on Christmas eve. In England, jellied eels are a delicacy. The Germans smoke them. The French eat eels, sometimes drowning them in wine, which supposedly improves the flavor by flooding the meat with adrenalin. The Spanish eat tiny eels as a delicacy. Both fresh water and sea eels are eaten by the Japanese, who broil them and coat them with a sweet sauce.

FUNGUS

Fungus to an American means athlete's foot. Mention it to an Italian and delicious mushrooms (a type of fungus) are evoked. A fungus is a sponge-like growth on another living thing, such as a tree trunk. Most fungi are asexual and devoid of chlorophyll, and some are poisonous. The delicious truffle is a fungus.

Chinese emperors, constrained by Buddhism from eating meat, had their chefs invent meat substitutes using fungi, nuts, and other ingredients. The most popular canned soup in China is called *White Fungus*. Mushroomburgers are available in some trendy urban restaurants for the gourmet vegetarian.

SEAWEED

Until recently, seaweed was available in the United States only in the form of a seasoning made of ground, dried kelp sold as a health food and salt substitute. The Japanese have eaten seaweed for centuries, treasuring its crunchy texture and unusual flavors and using it as a textural accent on food dishes. They also pound seaweed paper-thin and dry it, wrapping the crisp sheets around rice in sushi dishes. Dried seaweed keeps for years if protected from dust and moisture. When soaked in water it swells: a little goes a long way in the kitchen. The Kanembu tribe in Africa live on the shores of Lake Chad and eat *spirulina* algae, which they harvest from the lake, dry out, and make into a cake which they eat with tomatoes and chili peppers. Seaweed is nutritious and contains important substances such as iodine. It is not yet taken seriously in American kitchens and it awaits the innovations of chefs to come.

GUTS, STOMACHS, AND LUNGS

Haggis is a traditional Scottish dish made from sheep lungs, hearts, and livers. The ingredients are chopped with onions, spices and oatmeal, larded with suet (animal fat), and boiled in a container made from a sheep's stomach. It is an example of how an ethnic food is shaped by geography and history.

Scotland is sheep country. The organs and other cheaper parts of the sheep (called *garb*age in Medieval days) cost pennies and are loaded with vitamins, minerals, and other good nutritional things. The suet is easily burned up by the hard-working Scots, and the oatmeal makes it more palatable and balances the heavy protein of the other ingredients with the benefits of a wholesome grain much loved in Scotland.

The method of assembling and cooking the dish is a holdover from Medieval days when *bodings* (puddings), ancestors of modern sausages, were made by boiling the ingredients in animal stomachs or intestines. The cuisine of Scotland has never been noted for subtlety, but some Americans who eat haggis report an oddly satisfying taste. It is a dish which will never be served as *haute cuisine,* but one can get used to it, and even fond of it, over time.

TRIPE

The main ingredient of Mexican *menudo* is the stomach of a cow or other ruminant. This part of the animal is so despised as a food by Americans that the word has come to mean something offensive, worthless, contemptible, or inferior. The word comes from the Arabic *tharb,* meaning stomach, or net, a reference to the net-like appearance of a cow's stomach.

CREEPY-CRAWLIES

It is scary enough for the average American to have a hairy, many-legged creature crawling up an arm, but the thought of bringing a basket of them into the kitchen to make a stew is enough to cause retching and fainting, not to mention serious loss of appetite. In the film *Papillon,* the hero, played by Steve McQueen, demonstrated starvation in solitary confinement by eating a cockroach. The audience responded with a collective shudder.

Yet all over the world, insects, worms, slugs, lizards, snakes, and other repulsive (to Americans) creatures are downed with gusto. People who happily devour snails shrink in horror when offered sea slugs, a Chinese delicacy; yet the two creatures are similar. Tribes in South Africa roast termites until they are hard, then eat them like nuts. In New Caledonia the citizens dote on spiders, and the cockchafer beetle is eaten alive by little boys in Germany.

They are probably sold as a novelty joke, but it is possible to buy chocolate-covered ants, candied bees, pickled bull scrotum, and canned rattlesnake meat at certain specialty food stores in the United States and Europe. You won't find insects on the menu of the corner deli (at least, not *printed* on it), but it is permitted for orthodox Jews to eat grasshoppers, should anyone ever take it into their head. Leviticus 11:22 reads: "Of these you may eat the following: the common locust in its several species, the flying locust in its several species, and the grasshopper in its several species." Early Christians liked the flying bugs as well, as described in the Gospel according to Matthew. John the Baptist ate "locusts with wild honey," as he preached in the wilderness. The Prophet Mohammed also ate locusts, with relish.

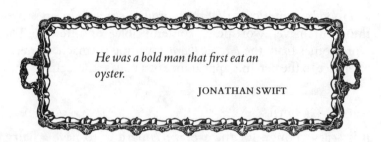

He was a bold man that first eat an oyster.

JONATHAN SWIFT

The late Gaylord Hauser was once asked his opinion on unbleached flour. The questioner stated that it often contained live insect eggs, as compared to bleached flour which contained chemicals that killed the eggs, but were also poisonous to the human system. What was his advice? the caller wanted to know. Hauser's reply was succinct:

"Poison can kill you," he said, "but insect eggs are pure protein."

SEA URCHINS

The sea urchin deserves a wider following in America than the sushi eaters who dote on it. It is popular in France and Chile, where it is marinated in lime juice and served with hot bread. The meat has a nut-like flavor and there are no bones or fat. The spiny sea urchin causes painful punctures for the swimmer unfortunate enough to step on one. When sea urchins' populations grow too large, they can lay waste to hundreds of square miles of undersea coral beds. They might be eaten for environmental reasons but principally because they are delicious— once you get used to them.

RATS AND MICE

In ancient China and India, mice were considered a delicacy. The god Apollo was said to consider mice sacred, so priests in old Greece occasionally ate them as a sacrifice to their god. The

Romans raised dormice as a gourmet item. They force-fed them on nuts and kept them in dark cages. The Roman dormouse was the size of a modern laboratory rat and was cooked by roasting, broiling, boiling, or frying. Honey and nuts were a favorite dressing. Gordon Liddy of Watergate fame is reported to have eaten a rat once to prove his toughness, but in Paris during the winter of 1870–1871, while the Prussians besieged the city, ladies and gentlemen ate rats in the finest restaurants, complete with truffles and champagne.

The Chef with a Conscience

One of the greatest of French chefs (yet almost unknown in France), a clothes horse, a show-off, a bit of a snob—Alexis Soyer was someone to remember: a genius and a hero in a profession not celebrated for heroism. Born in France in 1809, he lived only forty-nine years, but he packed several lifetimes in that brief span. Soyer spent most of his life in England and became more English than the English. So prominent as a character and wit was he that Thackeray based the French chef, Mirobolant, in his novel *Pendennis,* on Soyer.

Soyer invented dozens of sauces, many packaged and sold by his friends, Crosse and Blackwell. He invented a field stove for the military, designed kitchens for the Royal navy, and created dozens of gizmos, gadgets, and systems for the kitchen. He designed the kitchens for the Reform Club and was head chef there for many years, creating lavish meals for the members.

He could put on a feast for a thousand people or an intimate dinner for two. In one celebrated instance he roasted an entire ox by gas for the Royal Agricultural Society at Exeter in 1850. Quite capable of creating the most expensive dinners in England, he experimented with cheap and nourishing food for the poor, inventing a nutritious soup that could be made for pennies per quart. In 1847 Soyer went to Ireland during the terrible potato famine and opened soup kitchens.

At Christmas his dinners for the wealthy were celebrations of lavish feasting comparable to the great banquets of the Medieval period. At the same time he poured his energies into Christmas dinners for twenty thousand poor Londoners. He was sent to the Crimea by the government in 1855 to bring order to the unsanitary hospital kitchens. He worked there, side by side with Florence Nightingale, day and night until his health began to crack, contributing to his early death.

In addition to his other skills, Soyer was a talented writer of books about cooking. His first book, *The Gastronomic Regenerator,* was revolutionary, devising a new system of cooking aimed at the wealthy but also the lower economic classes. He included in the book plans for simple kitchens that could be built by people with little money.

As his zeal to spread the benefit of good cooking increased, he began visiting kitchens of various institutions and countless private homes in all economic classes, to see for himself what their problems were and how he might help them to prepare and eat good food. In 1849 he wrote *Modern Housewife,* or *Menagere,* slanted to the requirements of the middle class and written in the form of letters between two women, Hortense and Eloise.

In 1854 he wrote *Shilling Cookery for the People,* a bestseller, which sold 250,000 copies within a few years. Soyer was an odd and complex personality, combining the self-centered egotism of a Victorian dandy with a deep passion for the common person and an urge to put his skills at the disposal of everyone, regardless of class or financial condition, a cause which ultimately cost him his life.

The Count from Massachusetts

Those inquiries which lead to improvements by which the providing of food may be facilitated are matters of the highest concern to mankind.
Count Benjamin Rumford

Benjamin Thompson (1753–1814) was a teen-age terror, the

kind that turns a parent's hair prematurely gray. He nearly electrocuted himself when he duplicated Benjamin Franklin's kite experiment. He almost blew himself up experimenting with fireworks and was dismissed as a clerk in a dry goods store because he was always under the counter building a model or piece of equipment or reading a book about science instead of waiting on customers.

He was born on a farm near Woburn, Massachusetts, thirty miles from the farm where John Chapman, better known as Johnny Appleseed, was born twenty-one years later. Like Benjamin Franklin, he was a politician, inventor, and the toast of Europe, with a weakness for amorous exploits. Like Franklin, he is famous for inventing a stove, the first designed using scientific principles. He was the founder of home economics—the application of scientific principles to domestic management, the preparation of food, and the efficient feeding of people—and an ingenious inventor of dozens of devices to make life easier and more enjoyable. He spent his life devising schemes, experimenting, and inventing; advancing the abilities of people to overcome adversity, improve their health, and enjoy their lives.

While on a tour of Europe, he was hired as adviser to Prince Carl Theodor, elector of Bavaria, and given broad powers to reform the army and solve the problem of what to do with the beggars plaguing Munich. He put the soldiers to work in a factory making uniforms, and farming large gardens where they raised the food used by the army. He made the Bavarian army a respected model of self-sufficiency, established the first state-run public school system and, that done, rid the streets of dangerous beggar gangs by establishing compulsory workhouses where they learned a trade, got an education, and reentered society as productive citizens.

The clothing and feeding of the army and the experiment with the beggars led to Thompson's life-long concern with eliminating starvation and the efficient preparation of food. His interests turned to nutrition and he began the first scientific studies of diet: how to get balanced nourishment with the least expense. He believed soup was the most nourishing food. Using rigid scientific methods he invented a series of soups based on barley, potatoes and peas, accompanied by hard toast (to encourage slower eating), that enabled masses of people to be nourished at minimal expense. Soup kitchens were set up all over Bavaria and Thompson was soon called upon by Ireland, Poland, and other countries to help combat starvation.

His Bavarian patron made Thompson a Count of the Holy Roman Empire in 1792. Thompson chose the name Rumford, the former name of Concord, New Hampshire, where he began his spectacular rise to fame as a schoolteacher. For the rest of his remarkable life he was known as Count Rumford.

In those days, food was cooked on an open fire in a fireplace. Thompson noted the heat lost in this process which, "cooked the cook more than the food," and devised a cabinet to contain the fire—a large box whose top was used to heat food. This device, the first kitchen range, revolutionized the preparation of food and is one of his greatest accomplishments. In the process he invented the fireplace damper and redesigned the fireplace so the smoke went up the chimney instead of into the house. All modern fireplaces are based on his design. He discovered the principle of convection, used widely today.

Poems about him appeared in the press ("Lo, every parlour drawing room, I see, Boasts of thy stoves and talks of naught but thee."), songs were written in his honor, and he was invited to important functions.

In addition to the kitchen range, he invented the double boiler, the baking oven, different types of tea kettles, the fireless cooker, and he promoted the use of the pressure cooker. He laid the foundation for the techniques of cooking and baking in use today and profoundly affected the preparation of food worldwide. He was the first to advocate drip coffee and invented several types of drip machines, as well as the first portable coffee-maker. He was the first to drill holes in pot handles so they could be hung up, the first to design pot lids that helped the food cook better, the first to analyze fuels and manage heat scientifically, the first to study the processes of roasting, baking, and boiling, and to design kitchens based on their cooking function. His studies of stove insulation led to the work of others who applied his ideas to different fields.

He pioneered in studies of light and heat, guns and explosives, ship design, and many other areas, including the first concept of folding beds, and a hand-pushed lawn mower. His studies of heat resulted in his invention of the first steam radiator, an advance that spread quickly around the world. He conceived the idea of an American military academy, but was denied a role in establishing West Point because of his British sympathies during the Revolution.

Despite his wide-ranging interests he is best remembered as the Leonardo da Vinci of the kitchen, the wizard who revolutionized the preparation of food and turned it from a haphazard collection of customs and recipes into a scientific process subject to the disciplines and progress inherent in scientific inquiry.

Perhaps it was his siding with the Tories during the Revolution, or his notoriety as a spy for the British, or his numerous love affairs, or his penchant for exaggerating the truth to cast himself in a favorable light, or his never-ending arrogance and self-promotion, or a prejudice in favor of scientists who work in more glamorous disciplines; but he is a forgotten giant today, a footnote, an unheroic hero.

There are few people in the world today whose lives have not been touched by the work of Count Rumford. Every student in a "home ec" course, every cook that uses a stove, everyone who enjoys a balanced meal, owe something to this unusual human. In 1854, two scientists, one of them Eben Horsford, a professor who held the Rumford Chair of Applied Science at Harvard University, inspired by Rumford, founded a company whose purpose it was to invent baking powder, which they did in 1859. The count was long dead by then, but the innovative life he led was an inspiration to other scientists and continues to the present day (and the Rumford Company of Terre Haute, Indiana, is still manufacturing baking powder today, with a picture of the Count on each can). Although he achieved fame and wealth, and made major contributions to the advancement of civilized life, his greatest prize, immortality, somehow eluded him.

Sauerkraut-by-the-Sea

A German immigrant in New York City in the 1880s named Charles Feltman is generally credited with introducing the frankfurter into the United States. In the American tradition of the poor but industrious immigrant, Feltman started by selling pies from a pushcart in Coney Island. When the new hotels-being built opened their dining rooms, Feltman's business dropped, so he took on a new line: frankfurter sandwiches. He soon had enough money to open his own restaurant, Feltman's German Beer Garden.

Feltman's frankfurters were made of chuck beef and lean pork, with added pork fat for juiciness, pepper, salt, sugar, nutmeg, ginger, paprika, and corcandes, a Ceylonese spice. The mixture was stuffed into a thirteen-foot-long small intestine of a sheep, twisted and cut into five-and-a-half-inch frankfurters, and smoke-cured over a hickory fire. They were then cooked several times in water heated to 175 to 190 degrees Fahrenheit.

The finished sausage was sizzled on a hot griddle, served in a warm bun garnished with home-made mustard and sauerkraut, and washed down with a mug of ice-cold foamy beer from the tap, or a cherry soda. The hot dog sold for ten cents, the soda was three cents, the beer five cents. The all-beef frankfurter, a later development, was touted as an improvement, but was really a marketing ploy designed to appeal to Jewish customers who didn't want to eat anything made of pork. The kosher frank was an improvement on the all-beef version because it removed all doubt with its kosher seal and implied, to the non-kosher customer, that it was somehow purer than its predecessors. It was about this time (the 1920s) that the word *kosher* entered the English language in America to mean something whose authenticity was above reproach, strictly legal and above-board.

The hard-working Feltman built a mini-empire with hotel, beer gardens, restaurants and food stands, and various rides to amuse his customers. At his death in 1910 he left a business worth over one million dollars, a lot more money in those days than today, to his two sons, Charles L. and Alfred, and his grandson, Charles A. Feltman.

On a boiling-hot summer day in 1915 Nathan Handwerker, the manager of a small restaurant in Manhattan, decided to take the day off and went to Coney Island. A sign in Feltman's window said Help Wanted. On a whim, the young man wandered in. He spent the rest of the day slicing rolls for frankfurters and never went back to his old job in Manhattan.

The gregarious Handwerker made friends with two musicians, a singing waiter named Eddie Cantor and a piano player named Jimmy Durante, whose songs and comic antics entertained Feltman's customers. They urged Handwerker to set up his own hot dog stand. He would get rich they told him; they would send their friends to buy Handwerker's hot dogs if he did. Feltman, a generous man, allowed his employees to eat all the hot dogs they wanted free, thus unwittingly financing his biggest future competitor.

With the money saved from a year of eating hot dogs for breakfast, lunch, and dinner, Handwerker saved three hundred dollars, enough to pay the rent on his new stand for many months. When questioned in later years about his love for his own food, Nathan bragged, "I'll gladly wrassle anyone who's been living on caviar and champagne for thirty-nine years."

Young Handwerker opened his stand in Coney Island in 1916 near the corner of Surf and Stillwell Avenues and called it *Nathan's*. He sold his hot dogs for five cents each, half the price his former boss sold them for, including bun, mustard, and sauerkraut if you wanted. "Nathan's was America's first fast-food restaurant," claims William Handwerker, Nathan's grandson, who oversees the daily operations of the vast business that grew from that first hot dog stand.

The optimistic sign above his stand proclaimed in three-foot high letters, "Follow the crowd to Nathan's." But the crowd passed Nathan's by, clutching their dimes on their way to Feltman's. How could anything so cheap be any good? Many of the immigrants arrived for their day at the beach with baskets and bags filled with jars of carefully wrapped food, suspicious of *any* food not made in their own kitchens. Nathan offered a free pickle with every five cent hot dog. Then he offered a free root beer. Still the crowds shuffled by from the subway exit to the beach without buying. Nathan was slowly going broke. Desperate measures were called for.

Nathan rounded up some vagrants and gave them free hot dogs if they ate them in front of his stand. The crowds went to the other side of the street to avoid passing the bums eating hot dogs at Nathan's. But Nathan wouldn't quit. He selected ten of the best-looking bums from his pool, had them washed, shaved and dressed in white jackets and trousers borrowed from a friend in the theatrical costuming business. He draped a prop stethoscope around the neck of each one of them and had them stand under a new sign as they ate their hot dogs. The sign read, "If doctors eat our hot dogs, you know they're good!" So many people stopped to buy hot dogs that day the police had to keep the sidewalks clear.

Feltman stood fast, refusing to lower his price to compete with Nathan's. Instead, he hired an expensive chef imported from the Roney-Plaza Hotel in Miami Beach, installed new rides, and successfully sold a hamburger garnished with a gardenia (Coney Island slang for onion, because it smelled so nice) for ten cents. It was the Roaring Twenties, and both competitors prospered.

Over a hundred million hot dogs went down each year at

Coney Island. Baseball star Babe Ruth was crowned hot dog champ when he ate twenty-four hot dogs at one sitting, eased down with a gallon of lemonade. This was only a slight exertion for the Sultan of Swat, who ate four or five hot dogs every day in his long career in baseball.

In 1929 the Depression struck, and the handwriting was on the wall for Feltman's. It was now no longer an option to bypass Nathan's five-cent dogs for Feltman's higher-priced model; people still came to Coney Island but they didn't have much money to spend. Feltman's business started a slow decline and Nathan's took the lead over his old employer and competitor.

Feltman's greatest day, never to be repeated, was probably July 23, 1939. The World's Fair had just opened. The King and Queen of England visited the United States earlier in the year, and were served hot dogs in the White House by President Franklin Roosevelt, who wanted the British royals to taste something uniquely American. Back in Coney Island, the local chamber of commerce staged a ceremony to honor Feltman, who first introduced the hot dog to this country.

Feltman's was sold seven years later. The new owners soon declared bankruptcy and the doors closed for good in 1954. Nathan's was going strong, and celebrated its one-hundred-millionth hot dog, with appropriate ceremony, on July 6, 1955. His annual turnover was six million hot dogs per year at the time. Since then the company has continued to prosper. Nathan's Famous is franchised around the country today and many groceries and supermarkets sell frozen hot dogs and knackwursts bearing the famous name.

One of Handwerker's employees, an attractive redhead named Clara Bowtinelli, was, in what has since become another American legend, discovered by a talent scout at Nathan's and went on to motion picture fame as Clara Bow. Handwerker dispensed wisdom as generously as he dispensed sauerkraut, although sometimes not as effectively. A handsome, athletic young man who had a job as a stilt-walker at Coney Island once came to him for advice. He was thinking of going to Hollywood to act in the movies. Nathan advised him to stay put. "You got a steady job here, with friends, a salary, and a future. Out there you'll be out of work and you won't know anybody. Don't be foolish," he admonished. Fortunately for movie-goers, Cary Grant ignored Nathan's advice and went to Hollywood.

Handwerker became rich and Nathan's became Nathan's Famous, a shrine to New Yorkers. The founder spent his declining years in retirement in Florida, where he was kept abreast of the latest news from Coney Island by visits from his large family. He is remembered by grandson William as a jolly man, always smiling, with a twinkle in his eyes. Thanks to Feltman and Handwerker, the hot dog had achieved its status as America's favorite snack, and became a star along with Clara Bow, Eddie Cantor, Jimmie Durante, and Cary Grant.

Chapter 6

How Food Comes to You

Every fruit has its secret.

D. H. Lawrence

Made in the U.S.A. (and Canada)

Maple sugar and maple syrup are made only in the United States, and parts of Canada. The Algonquins, Ojibways, Crees, and other American Indians of the northeast made maple syrup for centuries before the coming of the white man. The Algonquins called it *sinzibuckwud,* "drawn-from-the-wood." Sugar maple trees transplanted to Europe and elsewhere don't produce enough syrup, or to be precise, the sap boiled down to make syrup. European winters do not have the temperature swings or duration necessary for the production of large quantities of sap. The trees require a climate with a long period that goes from below freezing during the night to above freezing the next day, a condition common in New England and parts of Canada.

During the Napoleonic era and for some time afterward, various countries in Europe tried to establish sugar maple trees as a crop. Although sugar was produced successfully, it was never produced in sufficient quantities to make the experiment worthwhile. When cheap imported sugar cane and locally grown sugar beets proved more feasible, the sugar maple industry of Europe slowly vanished.

Sugar maple trees grow as far east as New Brunswick, as

far north as Quebec and Ontario, Canada, as far west as Wisconsin and Iowa, and as far south as the mountains of Virginia. Of the United States' crop of maple syrup, one third comes from Vermont, one third from upstate New York, and the rest from all the other states. Sugar maple trees grown outside these areas withhold the sweet sap.

During the nineteenth century maple sugar was thought by farmers in the United States and Europe to be the form of sugar that would come to dominate world trade, but the dream never materialized. Today, maple syrup production figures are declining. Syrup production is laborious, not amenable to mechanization, and profits are slim. It takes thirty-five to sixty years for a tree to grow to the right size for syrup production. During this period the maple farmer must maintain the woodlands and pay taxes on the land. They are, in effect, growing their grandchildren's inheritance.

The sap rises at the end of winter, when slushy rain and several feet of snow make it difficult to work in the forest. Each tree averages twelve gallons of sap per season. It takes about forty gallons of sap to make one gallon of pure maple syrup. The number of trees producing syrup is dwindling and new trees are not being planted at a rate to reverse the decline. Trees that grow alongside roads have been dying because of the salt used to keep ice off the roads in winter. Salty runoff can be neutralized by gypsum, so farmers fertilize the trees with ground-up scrap gypsum wallboard from building projects (providing also the ecological advantage of less trash in landfills).

Syrup makers favor the light-colored syrup, or fancy grade, with its delicate flavor. City-dwellers favor the darker, sweeter type, with a strong maple sugar flavor and high sugar content. Suburban consumers favor the medium amber type. The crop is sold out every year, with demand growing and supply shrinking. In 1990, Vermont brought in $10.5 million in revenues from maple syrup, with a total of 375,000 gallons. Although figures are not yet in, 1991 has been an excellent year, and the Vermont Department of Agriculture estimates production may rise to well above 500,000 gallons. The combined production for all of New England in 1990 was 565,000 gallons. New York State produced 249,000 gallons during the same period. The most recent figures available (1978) from other producing states, in gallons, are as follows: Pennsylvania, 42,000; Ohio, 65,000; Michigan, 80,000; Wisconsin, 110,000; Minnesota, 5,000; Maryland, 13,000.

Counterfeiters combine corn syrup and artificial maple flavor to make a cheap imitation that drives the price of real syrup down. Some of the phony syrup claims to be "100 percent pure maple syrup." Buyers can avoid being cheated by patronizing reliable stores, or buying direct from the producers. Most farmers will ship anywhere in the country. A list of maple syrup producers may be obtained by writing to the Department of Agriculture in any of the syrup-producing states.

With all the problems in growing, making, and selling maple syrup, why do farmers persist? Most don't rely on maple syrup entirely, and tap the trees each year to supplement their farm income from other sources. But there's more to it than economics. Talk to maple syrup farmers and you'll hear phrases like, "the indescribable, wonderful smell of boiling sap," as one of them rhapsodized to me. He went on to describe the annual harvesting of the syrup as a joyous, community occasion, almost a mystical celebration of the coming of spring. He likened it to the Mardi Gras in New Orleans, an event involving almost everyone in the community in a traditional rite going back for centuries.

During the six weeks in March and April when the sap rises, the woods ring with laughter and good fellowship as school-bus drivers, teachers, school principals, veterinarians, plumbers, homemakers, bankers and lawyers join the farmers in tapping trees and boiling sap in their free time. Pouring boiled-down syrup onto fresh snow and eating the icy treat in the forest is a happy, wonderful experience, providing sweet memories for the children and their parents.

Mad Cows and Englishmen

The eating habits of an entire culture or nation are slow to change; people keep eating the same foods even though the initial reason for their preference is long gone. The pace of change in the modern world is forcing new eating patterns on us more and more rapidly. As government systems crumble and warfare, economics, technology, and communications cause traumatic cultural convulsions, eating does not escape. What we put into our stomachs depends on what is available.

Deer steak is now sold in many British supermarkets and restaurants. One reason for this change in the nation of the beefeater is the outbreak of mad-cow disease. Infected cows have fits of uncontrollable trembling and shuddering, rolling their eyeballs and falling down, shaking with seizures and must be destroyed. The disease lodges in the animal's brain, wreaking havoc in the nervous system.

Animal brains are a by-product of meat-packing plants, mainly utilized as food for other livestock. This thrifty-sounding idea backfired when it was learned that mad-cow disease was transmitted by this means. Fearful consumers stopped eating beef.

There are an estimated one million wild deer in Britain, about one-third of them in Scotland. Britain exports 80 percent of the 3,000 tons of wild venison harvested annually, mainly to West Germany, whose citizens love to eat game animals. Now that unification of Germany is a fact, East Germany, Hungary, and Poland have taken over this market, undercutting the British.

The price of wild venison in England dropped almost 60 percent since 1990. This is complicated by the preference of British buyers for farmed venison even though the wild variety is (presumably) healthier, free-range, and feeds on natural products. Farmed venison production has risen from 100 tons a year in 1987 to 500 tons a year in 1991. Much of the increased stock is sold to new deer farmers as breeding stock and will not reach the market for several years.

Britain's food habits are changing as a result of the mad-cow scare and the larger phenomenon of England's newly-awakening interest in gourmet eating and healthier food—a major development historically. Until recently, Britain seemed stuck on the broken record of Medieval puddings, roasts, and terrible bread, while the rest of Europe, led by France, pioneered new culinary frontiers.

As England pulls up a chair at the international gourmet table a return to the days of Robin Hood may be in the offing. With a million wild deer wandering about and the country in the midst of an economic downturn, the bowmen of Britain, once the scourge of Europe, may once again be on the prowl.

The Grains of Wrath

When Hernando Cortés invaded Mexico he obliterated the culture of the Aztec Indians, substituting Christianity and the morality of Spain and Europe. One of the casualties of this forced reculturation was *amaranth,* a grain considered sacred by the natives. What repelled Cortes was their habit of drinking it mixed with human blood in their rituals. They also made a paste of ground *amaranth* seeds, called *zoale,* and fashioned pagan figures from it, to the annoyance of their conquerors.

As they relieved the Indians of their gold, the Spaniards also denuded their *amaranth* farms, forbidding the cultivation of this heretical food. Anyone found growing or eating *amaranth* was immediately put to death. Eaten for over six thousand years, *amaranth* disappeared from Mexico overnight—although some Aztecs continued to grow the crop surreptitiously.

In the Andes, the Incas used another grain, *quinoa,* (pronounced, keen-WAH), as a sacred food. It followed the fate of *amaranth* when the Inca culture was destroyed in turn by Pizarro.

Today both grains are making a comeback. *Amaranth,* available in spinach-like leaf form or as grain, is increasingly popular with the health-food set and is used by *nouvelle cuisine* experimenters in place of spinach. It is loaded with natural calcium and iron and is a good source of protein.

Quinoa is destined for greater fame because it not only contains high amounts of protein, iron, and calcium, but also lysine, methionine, and cystine, three important amino acids. *Quinoa* is a good substitute for rice. It has potential for fighting starvation in developing countries as well as gracing the tables of upscale food fans.

Both *amaranth* and *quinoa* are superior to wheat in many of their nutritional values. Both have more protein than corn or barley, and both contain more than 6 percent lysine, an essential amino acid, as compared to less than 3 percent in wheat. Variations of both grains have been cultivated into modern times as far north as Illinois, and were used by the Pueblo Indians of New Mexico and the Navajos.

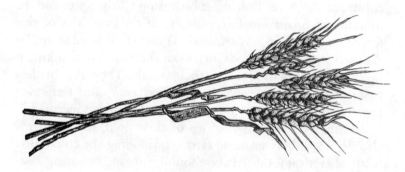

Going Against the Grains

Until the present preoccupation with wholesome foods got under way, all one had to know about grains was: rice is rice, wheat is wheat, corn is corn! Now the consumer faces a new and unfamiliar lineup in the market, and trying to make sense of the bewildering variety can sometimes be confusing. Here-

with, a short guide to a few of the new/old grains that promise
to improve your health and stimulate your appetite:

Blue corn has no magical ingredient making it healthier
than yellow or white corn. It is delicious, as corn meal goes,
and its blue color is a conversation starter. It is a genuine American
Indian food, still in use today, but imparts no particular
blessings to the eater.

Bulgar (or bulgur) is not a special grain imported from an
exotic land where they live to be one hundred years old by eating
it. It is ordinary wheat cracked into several pieces and
cooked whole to make tabbouleh or pilaf. It is considered
healthier than milled wheat because it retains most of the nutrients
and needs a shorter cooking time to prepare. It's a nice
substitute for rice or potatoes.

Graham flour is another name for whole wheat flour and
was named after the Reverend Sylvester Graham, who railed
against white flour from his New England pulpit one hundred
years ago; it took that long for his radical ideas to be accepted.
The graham cracker was named in his honor. (Graham was
also opposed to feather beds, corsets, tea, coffee, and masturbation.)

Buckwheat is a fruit masquerading as a grain. We accept its
little ruse and use it in cereals or roasted and cooked as *kashe,* a
hearty substitute for potatoes or rice. When ground into flour,
it is used to make pancakes and baked dishes. It is an old world
food from eastern Europe.

Semolina is a special flour ground from the heart, or *endosperm*
of durum wheat. It is favored for making pasta because
the chemical structure of semolina allows it to retain whatever
shape it is made into, and it will not dissolve when boiled.

Basmati rice is a long grain rice from India that cooks up
into a fluffy dish with a nutty taste. The type available in burlap
bags in ethnic markets has usually not been sprayed with
chemicals. As a result it contains dead insect pests, easily
rinsed away in the washing process, a small inconvenience to
exchange for pure food. If you find that objectionable, you can

buy basmati rice already cleaned and packaged in neat plastic or cloth bags (more expensive of course).

Millet is not wheat but a separate grain once found only in birdseed. It is now widely available and is the main ingredient of *injera,* the soft, spongy bread used to wrap around food made by the Ethiopians.

Bran is the coarse, outer coat of any cereal grain. Its protective toughness makes it an ideal intestinal scourer, an antidote for constipation. Bran is also the name of a Celtic god of the underworld, a mythical king of Britain, and a dog in Icelandic mythology; fitting company for a grain element that works wonders in the bowels of humanity. Now touted as a cancer preventive as well as an aid to regularity, bran is no Johnny-come-lately to the nutrition scene. Post's Bran Flakes were sold almost sixty years ago as an aid to regularity.

Stuff It!

Sweeney Todd, the demon barber of Fleet Street who made meat-pies of his unsuspecting customers, would have delighted in the apocryphal tales, common in America, of the strange things stuffed into frankfurters, salami, baloney, and other members of the sausage family. Horror stories of insect parts, rat droppings and other vermin leavings, not to mention less menacing fillers such as cereal, gristle, gelatin, water, fat, and even sawdust, turned out to be all-too-true in the past and led to the creation of the Food and Drug Administration and a host of laws to ensure a supply of wholesome food to the public.

Sausage-makers have some points in their favor when accused of adding bread crumbs and water to sausages. Modern machines churn out one-and-a-half miles of sausage per hour. The mixing machine blades turn so fast they get hot. Bacteria breed at eighty degrees Fahrenheit, so ice must be added to cool the mixture. Melted ice blends with the bread crumbs added to bind the meat so it doesn't turn lumpy, creating a smoother texture and swelling the sausage. But when nitrates, nitrites, monosodium glutamate, skim milk, soy protein, and other fillers and preservatives are added to stretch the meat content, preserve the product, enhance or add color, and artificially "improve" the taste, problems arise.

"If it's made by human hands don't buy it," caution food purists. Yet a sausage made with quality meat properly spiced is a treat beyond compare. Like many foods, the origins of the ubiquitous sausage are lost. The word comes from the Latin *salsus,* a concoction made with the earliest preservative *sal,* "salt." Early sausage-making was a method of preserving meat by adding salt and spices to ground meat and stuffing it into animal gut, the only airtight container available to early civilizations, then cooking and smoking the finished product for further preservation, creating a delicious treat. The Old English *boding* "pudding" was animal gut filled with spiced blood or meat, and *boded* well for those who would eat its tasty contents. This ancestor of the modern sausage spread across

Europe in Medieval times. The onomatopoeic word *sausage* conjures the sizzle and smell of a plump and fragrant sausage on a grill, oozing juices, crisp skin ready to pop with the first pressure of a knife.

Milk Becomes Immortal

It's not hard to imagine how butter was discovered. It probably happened soon after cows were first domesticated in Turkey or Macedonia, around 6300 B.C. (According to an early frieze the farmer originally sat behind the cow to milk it, rather than on the side as today. The unpleasant view, the danger from kicking, and the risk of things dropping into the milk, or onto the milker, no doubt soon changed that practice.)

One day, an unsung nomad decided to take a load of milk to the next village and used a goatskin water bag to carry it on the back of his camel. As the milk sloshed back and forth inside the bag the equivalent of churning took place. When he arrived there was a mass of golden, delicious fat inside the bag.

The discovery of butter was amazing but had some drawbacks. It wasn't a food by itself and had to be mixed into, or spread on something to make it palatable. It lasted longer than milk, but not by much, and it quickly melted in hot climates. Tibetans got around the problem by developing a taste for rancid butter; other societies added salt as a preservative.

The story hardly finishes there. On the day some other nomad decided to ferry a load of milk and discovered that the supply of goatskin bags had vanished, milk took the leap to immortality. The nomad couldn't skin and cure a goatskin fast enough to make a bag in time to take the milk to the next village, but a sheep's stomach would suffice and could be utilized as soon as it was removed from a freshly-slaughtered animal.

When he arrived and opened the bag he discovered that instead of butter, a white, curdled mass had congealed inside. It tasted good and was not greasy like butter. He poured it into a basket to drain it, pressed the rest of the liquid out, and gave the first cheese-tasting party in history. The difference was the presence of rennin, an enzyme secreted by the mucous lining of the fourth stomach of a ruminant (like cows, for example), and which is essential to curdling milk and transforming it into cheese. When left in a cool place the cheese hardened on the outside, thereby preserving the inside. When cheese did spoil, it was often attacked by bacteria whose growth made the cheese taste even better.

Cheese-making spread around the world and became a valued staple of most civilizations. David was bringing ten loaves of cheese to the Hebrew army when he encountered the Philistine strong-man, Goliath, a subtle reference to the strength-building attributes of cheese. When Job argued with God about his afflictions, he used a cheesy analogy to make his point, "Hast thou not poured me out like milk, and curdled me like cheese?"

The ancient Greek god Aristaeus was worshiped for his gift of cheese, which was fed to Olympic athletes daily to increase their strength. Citizens on the island of Delos, where many Olympic games were held, imprinted pictures of cheese on their coins. Greek children were given presents of small cheeses when they were good, as were Roman children. When Odysseus and his men entered the cave of Cyclops, the one-eyed giant strong man, they discovered a storehouse of cheese which they promptly ate. Cheese was a valuable export and trade commodity all around the Mediterranean.

When England was a province of Rome, the city of Chester was noted for its fine cheese. The Romans built a wall around the town to protect it. Cheshire cheese was made in a mold shaped like a cat, later made famous as the smiling feline in *Alice In Wonderland*.

Pliny the Elder (A.D. 23 to 74) told about *Caseus Helveticus,* (Swiss cheese), in his classic *Natural History,* in which he also describes a Nîmes cheese "that bears away the prize," a possible reference to an early version of Roquefort. When

Charlemagne (742 to 814) stopped to visit a monastery in Aveyron, France, it was a fast day. The only food on hand to offer the emperor was a piece of the local cheese, a Roquefort. As the emperor carefully scraped away the blue mold, the bishop politely informed him that he was throwing away the tastiest part. He gingerly tasted the veins and was so impressed he ordered the monks to supply him with two loads of the moldy cheese every year. In gratitude to the monks, he gave them a farm he owned before he left town.

The first law to protect the cheese industry was enacted in 1411, when Charles VI gave the people of Roquefort "the monopoly of curing cheese as has been done in the caves of Roquefort village since time immemorial."

Cheese Highlights

Cheese is such a vast subject that to do it justice would require an entire book, which several people have already written. The history of cheese is filled with fascinating stories. Herewith a few.

1620—The Pilgrims land at Plymouth Rock, bringing cheese with them as part of the cargo.

1790—Marie Harel makes Camembert cheese. Camembert was possibly created before this date, but the French, who take cheese seriously, credit her as the inventor. There are two monuments to Madame Harel in France (and one in Ohio). Napoleon is said to have named the cheese after the town in northwest France where it is made. When he first tasted it he was so delighted he kissed the waitress who brought it to him.

1801—Thomas Jefferson's admirers gave him a huge cheese for his inauguration as president.

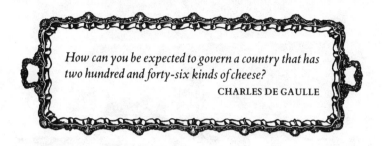

> *How can you be expected to govern a country that has two hundred and forty-six kinds of cheese?*
>
> CHARLES DE GAULLE

1829—Not to be outdone, Andrew Jackson's admirers gave *him* a huge cheese at *his* inauguration, about three feet high and over six feet in diameter, to judge from a drawing of the event. He left it in the entry hall at the White House, where his friends made short work of it.

1815—A group of Trappist monks returned to France after having been exiled by Napoleon and reopened their monastery, which they gratefully named their "port of salvation." The cheese they invented upon their return bears the name of the monastery, *Port-du-Salut.* In the same year, the Congress of Vienna convened. After the delegates re-arranged the countries of Europe, the next priority was cheese. Brie was voted "The King of Cheeses," under the instigation of Tallyrand.

1851—The world's first cheese factory opened near Rome, New York, making cheddar. By 1865 there were five hundred cheese factories in New York state. By 1869 two-thirds of all the cheese made in the United States came from factories.

1877—John Jossi invented American Brick cheese in Wisconsin.

1892—A Swiss cheese-maker, Emil Frey, in Monroe, New York, invents a new type of cheese while unsuccessfully trying to duplicate a German cheese, Bismarck Schlosskase. He named it after his glee club, The Liederkrantz (wreath of song). The cheese was such a spectacular success they quickly

outgrew the small factory in New York and decided to build a brand new factory in Van Wert, Ohio. When they started to produce Liederkrantz in the new plant it was tasteless. After much head-scratching someone had a brainstorm. The old factory in New York was taken apart and brought to Ohio, where the smelly, mold-covered shelves and equipment was scraped off. The crud from the old factory was smeared over the walls and the new equipment in Ohio and, magically, the cheese regained its flavor and was able to be reproduced in the new plant.

1901—The French invent Double Creme cheese (60 percent butterfat). Triple Cremes were invented by the French in the 1950s, containing 75 percent butterfat. At about the same time the French invented Double Creme cheese, American Cream Cheese was invented simultaneously in two different parts of New York State. Ironically, it was named after the city most popular in the United States at the time, Philadelphia.

1916—A cheese-maker named James L. Kraft learned how to pasteurize cheese and invented the first processed cheese.

1926—Dr. Joseph Knirim of New York City went to Vimoutiers, France, to tell the manufacturers of Camembert cheese about his new cure for stomach ailments. He found that patients with such problems were often cured completely when fed a diet of pilsner beer and Camembert cheese. It was subsequently discovered that Camembert contains a mold similar to penicillin, discovered years later by Alexander Fleming.

Yearly per capita consumption of cheese in the United States in 1987 was twenty-four pounds.

The Fishy Resurrection

The sushi chef cuts away several slices of giant clam as the customer watches approvingly. Before dipping into the vinegared-rice pot to fashion little platforms for the fishy morsels, he raps them smartly with the side of his knife. Like the splintered broom in *The Sorcerer's Apprentice,* the slices move slightly, as if trying to come back to life, proving to the customer that the clam was fresh.

Fresh fish is the sushi imperative; no Japanese will patronize a restaurant that cannot provide it. Shipping live fish in tanks of seawater from the docks to the big cities of Japan is not only costly because of the weight of the water, but dangerous. A few drops of seawater on the aluminum parts of an airplane can cause corrosion and crashes.

Japanese scientists solved the dilemma using *anabiosis,* a phenomenon first observed in 1720 by Anton van Leeuwenhoek, the inventor of the microscope, who noticed tiny animals and plants thought dead come back to life when moistened. Instead of drying the fish, the Japan Air Lines (JAL) team of scientists lowered their body temperature almost to freezing. The fish went into a state of suspended animation. Their bodies became stiff and their gills stopped functioning.

Several hours later the seemingly dead fish were placed in a tank of seawater at room temperature and quickly came back to life. Fish are now routinely shipped live all over Japan with only a little ice keeping them at the right temperature until they can be delivered, live and wriggling, to the happy chefs. Fish in the suspended state will live for ten days before being revived.

Waiter, There's a Nest in My Soup!

If soup made from the nest of a bird sounds strange, the reality is stranger still.

The source of this odd Chinese culinary specialty is the swiftlet, a tiny bird which makes its nest from strands of gummy saliva secreted by extra-large glands under its tongue. The nests are affixed to the slippery rocks of cave walls in remote places. The strands harden when exposed to air and bond to the rock. Unlike other birds which make nests from twigs and straw and need a branch or ledge to support them, the do-it-yourself swiftlet chooses sheer, vertical rock surfaces. Its lightweight nests are immune to every predator except man.

The swiftlet finds its way inside pitch-black caves using a form of echolocation similar to the bat, makes its nest, lays eggs, raises the family, and abandons the nest. Human harvesters climb to the cave ceilings using bamboo ladders and poles built centuries ago and kept in repair by generation after generation of nest harvesters.

Hundreds of feet above the cave floor they pry the nests off the sheer walls using a special tool with alleged magical powers. If they don't use this tool, they believe it will anger the gods that protect the birds and they, the harvesters, will fall to their deaths. With one hand holding the flimsy support and a flaming torch held between their teeth to see what they are doing, the daredevils reach out over the void and pluck the nest away. One miscalculation and they plunge to the cave floor. Many die each year. Those who are successful have a serene, zen-like concentration and the sure-footedness of a high-wire artist.

Harvesters are preyed on by pirates and robbers. Each team protects itself with guns, shooting it out with any thieves who appear. A harvester collects fifty nests a day for an overseer who arrives periodically to take the nests, pay the men, and give them food and gifts. Overseers are licensed by their governments—a sort of franchise fee—and allowed to harvest nests for a limited period.

The nests are washed, picked clean of foreign matter, and sold to restaurants who serve them simmered in chicken broth for fifty dollars a bowl. To the western palate the nest is tasteless and rubbery. To the aficionado it is heavenly. Perhaps part of the appeal is the reputation of bird's nest soup as an aphrodisiac. Some restaurants coyly deceive their American clientele by selling bird's nest soup in which the nest is nothing more than some noodles fashioned into a nest-like wreath. If the price-per-bowl isn't astronomical, chances are it's a fake.

From Indonesia to Hong Kong, the market for white nests is $20 million per year, selling for $1,800 per pound. The market for the desirable white nests are supplemented by smaller markets for the cheaper black nests (which contain feathers), and the red nests, colored by the blood of the bird or the minerals in the rock, depending on which expert you talk to. This unusual food is harvested from caves in Thailand, Indonesia, Burma (Myanmar), Malaysia, Vietnam, and the Philippines.

Hong Kong is the biggest buyer: 60 percent of the world harvest goes to their happy gourmets. Chinese communities in North America take another 30 percent and mainland China imports 10 percent of the Hong Kong market.

Swiftlet nests have been a Chinese delicacy for fifteen hundred years. The Chinese believe they are salutary for lung ailments, skin rejuvenation, and good for young children, convalescents, and the elderly. The nests contain a water-soluble glycoprotein that promotes cell division in the immune system. The medical profession is researching bird nest glyco. If they can isolate and identify the active ingredient it may have potential for treatment of immune system disorders.

They had better hurry. The swiftlet population is declining due to over-harvesting.

Mysterious Mushrooms, Tantalizing Truffles

Of all the world's foods, the strangest are mushrooms, for centuries associated with witchcraft. The ancient Greeks attributed the mushroom's overnight growth to lightning striking the ground.

Their colors range across the palette, from the glowing yellow of the chanterelle, to the pale sepia of *Agaricus bisporus*, the common grocery-store mushroom, to the shrouded black horn-of-plenty, called *trompettes-des-morts* (death's trumpets) by the French. Some mushrooms are violet, purple, or shades of blue, while others present themselves in delicate porcelain hues; some have lovely velvet surfaces and others seem to have been painted in bright auto enamels by a graffiti madman. Some are dry and brittle and others ooze slimy secretions. The strawberries-and-cream mushroom, which looks exactly as its name suggests, drips bright red sap onto the ground as if it were bleeding.

The mysterious god Soma of the ancient Aryan religion is believed to have been the hallucinogenic *fly-agaric* mushroom, whose fire-engine-red head speckled with white warts makes it a standout. The poisonous *fly agaric* may be eaten under certain circumstances, if properly prepared. It was used in shamanic ceremonies until recent times by Siberian tribesmen. Eating wild mushrooms can be deadly. They should never be eaten, or sometimes even touched, until they have been identified by an experienced mycologist (mushroom expert).

Mushrooms flourish in the dark. They are not green because they don't need chlorophyll or sunlight to grow, and have
no leaves, roots, flowers, or seeds. Their appearance is often
stunning, from the vaulted, arched ribs of the chantarelle, to
the closely-packed fins under the common mushroom's cap, to
the honeycombed morel and the ostrich-egg-sized giant puffball; they are wonders of natural design.

They reproduce by discharging huge quantities of microscopic spores into the air, which float around until they land in
a hospitable environment, where they begin the process of reproduction. A growing mushroom is a powerhouse. Mushrooms have lifted loaded barrels of wine off winery floors,
pushed through three inches of asphalt, and cracked floors
made of solid concrete.

The mushroom is perhaps the most fertile plant in the
world. Albert Pilat, a Czech biologist, estimated that a large
puffball he examined produced 1.5 trillion spores. Placed end
to end, the spores from this one mushroom would encircle the
earth fifteen times. An ordinary meadow mushroom can produce 1.8 billion spores. They impregnate the earth; they are
everywhere, awaiting the opportunity to grow. As you read
these lines you are inhaling mushroom spores, your clothing is
laden with them, they cover your shoes. Your body is sprinkled with spores from mushrooms far away, all awaiting the
right conditions for growth.

When a spore lands in hospitable soil it forms *mycelium,* the
threadlike underground mushroom plant. In places where soil
nutrients are evenly distributed, the *mycelium* sometimes forms
a circle. After a good downpour, the *mycelium* sends up a circu-
lar ring of mushrooms, the fairy circle of folk tales which
proved that fairies had danced on that spot the night before.
Once established, such rings continue to grow and expand.
Fairy rings six hundred feet in diameter that pre-date the land-
ing of Columbus have been found in Kansas. In England fairy
rings found near Stonehenge give evidence to the faithful that
something magical is going on there.

Many mushrooms are so delicious they are sought by connoisseurs. Others contain within their soft meat deadly poisons which can kill anything that eats them. Their mysterious nature, and the resemblance of some mushrooms to a phallus have given them the reputation of aphrodisiacs, although the only passions they can demonstrably arouse are gustatory.

A few mushrooms are funny fellows, such as the *cepe,* called *porcini* in Italy for their resemblance to little pigs. With their coolie-style caps and stems bulging at the bottom, they resemble the dancing mushrooms in Walt Disney's film, *Fantasia.*

The most precious mushroom in the world is the truffle, not a mushroom at all, but a fungus that grows underground on oak tree roots (except for those which are mined. Deep in the Kalihari Desert of Botswana, in southern Africa, are truffle mines containing some of the richest troves of the valuable food in the world.) The Perigord, the black truffle of France, is considered by many gourmets to be the finest. Second is the white Piedmontese truffle, called "the white diamond," because of its expense. Truffles were eaten in Babylon and ancient Rome, where they were thought to be made of an earthy substance, balled together, according to Pliny the Elder.

At first, truffles were considered an aphrodisiac, the mistaken historical role of many new foods. According to legend, in 1368 the Duke of Clarence married a woman in Italy whose dowry included several truffle-laden hills around Alba. At the wedding feast the Duke primed himself to consummate his marriage by gorging on his new wife's truffles. He died of overeating that night before he could discover if the truffles were aphrodisiacal.

Truffles are hunted traditionally by pigs or dogs. Pigs are preferred because of their unique ability to smell the truffle's scent and root them out; but pigs are pigs and like to eat the truffles they find. Dogs are not as efficient at finding truffles but have better manners than their porcine colleagues. In 1810 a patient and observant French peasant named Joseph Talon discovered how to farm truffles by planting acorns from truffle-rich oak trees in other areas known to produce truffles, and waiting; it takes six to ten years before truffles appear in a new location.

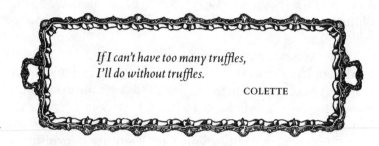

> *If I can't have too many truffles,*
> *I'll do without truffles.*
>
> COLETTE

The more than five thousand varieties of mushrooms in the United States can be classified as edible, inedible (bitter, tasteless, unchewable, etc., but not poisonous), and poisonous. Of the approximately one hundred poisonous species, less than a dozen can cause death. An estimated twelve people die in the United States each year from poisonous mushrooms, about the same number that die from snake bites. Accurate figures are not available, and there are undoubtedly unreported illnesses and deaths caused by toxic mushrooms that are attributed to other causes. The world-wide estimate for deaths from poisonous mushrooms, according to one source, is between twenty and three hundred per year.

The cultivated mushroom, *Agaricus bisporus,* is the most familiar mushroom to Americans, found in almost every grocery store in neat, plastic-wrapped baskets. Field mushrooms are sold in some gourmet stores and are worth experimenting with. Some of the more common of the exotic mushrooms are the meadow mushroom, one of the oldest to be eaten, called *mussiriones* by the Franks of northern France. The word *mushroom* is derived from the Frankish word.

The French morel, which looks like a small sponge, is imported dried or canned, as is the Italian porcini. The French chanterelle is available fresh in some markets. Asiatic grocery stores usually stock a variety of unusual fresh, dried, or canned

Oriental mushrooms. Most popular are the shiitake from Japan and China, the straw mushroom, the oyster mushroom, and the enoki from Japan, a tiny, long-stemmed yellow mushroom with a small cap. Other mushrooms available in the United States are the wood ear from China, and the matsutake from Japan.

The American morel is found all along the Canadian border and as far west as California, but grows most abundantly in Michigan, where the annual spring mushroom hunt has a uniquely American character. Hunters can stay at the Mushroom Cap Motel in Meswick, and relax after a hard day in the woods at the Mushroom Bar. There are four different morel festivals in Michigan each year. The elusive morel can bring $25 a pound fresh, and $15 to $20 an ounce dried. That comes to $320 per pound, about the same price as the dried French imported morels. "You can always tell a morel hunter," says one local, "they walk like Groucho Marx." The bent-over morel hunters bring more money into Michigan each year than all the duck and deer hunters put together.

Thomas Jefferson and a long line of American mycologists since him have tried unsuccessfully to raise morels. In 1987, a Michigan company called Neogen finally discovered the technique, which they are keeping secret. Morel Mountain, a subsidiary of Domino's Pizza, now licenses the process from Neogen, and produces approximately four tons of morels per year, with a retail value of $2,560,000. Farm-grown morels are claimed to be as good as the wild variety, with the added advantages of being picked at the height of maturity and flavor and delivered to eager gourmets clean and bug-free.

Other mushrooms are available only to those who go into the woods and hunt for them: the parasol mushroom (found along sea shores), the fairy-ring mushroom, the puffball, the lawyer's wig (or inky cap mushroom) which grows alongside roads, the wood-blewit (found under various trees), and the green cap (found in beech woods). The grisette, a gray-capped delight found under beech trees and much prized in France, the rubber brush, named after its spines, and the horn of plenty are also among collector's favorites.

From an optional topping on a pizza pie to the *pièce de résistance* of a gourmet feast, the mysterious mushroom is gaining popularity as one of America's favorite foods.

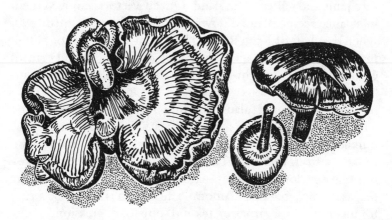

Please Eat the Daisies

When you eat broccoli, cauliflower, and artichokes, or sprinkle capers into a salad, you are eating flowers—or at least their buds. Some upscale grocers feature baby zucchini with the flower still attached. They have an intriguing flavor in salads and omelets. Some stores sell flowers you can toss in a salad, but they are still a novelty. The thought of eating flowers has overtones of eccentricity.

Such prejudices didn't bother our ancestors. Nicander the poet wrote of rose-flavored water 140 years before Christ. Apicius, the cookbook writer of old Rome, calls for violets, roses, mallow flowers, and flower bulbs in some of his recipes. Rose water is a common flavoring in the Mid-East today, giving candy, ice cream, pastry, and meats a light and pleasant taste. Orange, lemon, and lime blossoms are also used in the Mediterranean area. Italians flavor Sambucca with elder flowers, and a twig of flowers is inserted in each bottle of Fiore de Italia before it is sealed. Chartreuse is flavored with carnations by the Carthusian monks who make the liqueur.

Rose hips are a popular source of vitamin C, and are made into jams and jellies in England. Queen Victoria enjoyed them in a sauce recipe handed down in the royal house since 1390, when the chefs of King Richard II compiled the first cookbook in the English language, *The Forme of Cury,* ("The Form of Cookery") The straight-laced Victorians nibbled candied violet petals in their salons.

Flowers flavored salads, puddings, tarts, custards, liqueurs, and candies in Europe for centuries. They were eaten raw, pulped, fried, and used in stuffing fowl. The Chinese, who make tea from roots and flowers as well as tea leaves, use jasmine, roses, lotus, peonies, narcissus, and marigolds to make tea, as do the Japanese. Camomile flower tea is said to be a cure for insomnia, and carnation tea and soup for depression.

Flowers, with their wild beauty and connection with the mysteries of reproduction, were often associated with magic, sorcery, and witchcraft. A popular brew of flowers in the Middle Ages was said to enable one to see the fairies, an early form of mind-altering substances. With their delicate flavors and wild colors, flowers add poetry to food.

For experimenting, use those you grow or buy from a herbalist or food supplier; commercially grown flowers may have harmful insecticides on them. Certain flowers are toxic and should be avoided. If in doubt, consult a herbalist or other expert on the subject. Flowers may be eaten fresh, or dried for later use.

Here's a partial list of edible flowers:

Acacia, apple (or any fruit flower), borage (leaves and flowers), camomile, carnations, clover, cowslips, elder flowers, hawthorn, hibiscus, hollyhocks, jasmine, lavender, lilacs, lime flowers, marigolds, mimosa, nasturtiums, orange flowers, pinks, primroses, roses (petals and hips), rosemary flowers, thyme flowers, violets, zucchini flowers (or any squash flower).

The A, Bee, and C of Honey

For he on honey-dew hath fed
And drunk the milk of Paradise.
   Kubla Kahn
    Samuel Taylor Coleridge

Flowers and bees first appeared in the Miocene Age, ten to twenty million years ago. When the Ice Age ended ten thousand years ago, records of honey-gathering appeared on cave walls. The Promised Land of the Bible overflowed with milk and honey—symbols of abundance. The Egyptians revered honey as a magical substance; jars of it were found in New Kingdom tombs circa 1400 B.C. In addition to its use as food, the Egyptians believed a spoonful of honey made the medicine go down—in fact it was the medicine. Of the nine hundred remedies prescribed by early Egyptian doctors, five hundred mention honey. Egyptians used honey as a preservative and embalmed bodies in it. Borrowing from the Egyptians, Alexander the Great's undertakers put his remains in a jug of honey. Honey found in Egyptian tombs had not spoiled after over two thousand years and was still edible. Honey is the only food which will not spoil. It does crystallize, but can be revived by heating.

Bees cannot penetrate the skin of plants and so get most of their nectar from the flowers. Other insects can puncture the plant's surface and suck the juices. They extract nutrients from the sap and excrete the residue on the plant where it is found by bees, who drink it and turn this honeydew into honey. Aristotle thought honeydew fell from the air and had something to do with rainbows. It must be the nectar of the gods, fallen to earth, he posited. Pliny the Elder thought it a sweet liquid of the heavens, saliva from the stars or juice produced when air purified itself.

Honey was finally recognized as a product bees made from flower nectar in the 1700s. When the early settlers brought bee hives to the New World the Indians called the bees "white man's flies," and dubbed the white clover grown for the bees, "white foot." Honey was an important crop, providing the only sugar the pioneers knew (until they found out about maple syrup).

The honeybee has long been a symbol of industriousness; there are so many hard-working people (and bees) in Utah it was dubbed "The Bee Hive State." The bee's reputation is well-earned. If all the travels of a colony of bees were added up, the equivalent of three orbits around the earth would be needed to produce one pound of honey. Bees must produce eight pounds of honey to provide one pound for harvesting, so the amount of flying to make a pound for the bee-keeper is equal to twenty-seven orbits of the earth.

The bee turns nectar into honey with enzymes secreted by its hypopharyngeal glands: diastase, invertase, and glucose oxidase. The invertase inverts the natural sugar of the plant (sucrose) and converts it to glucose and fructose, boosting the sugar content of honeydew and transforming it into honey. The bee transfers the droplets to other bees and in the handling, water evaporates, condensing the honey into a thick syrup.

Bees function according to a program entered into their chromosomes millions of years ago. As a result, odd things sometimes occur. Bees that lived near a raspberry-jam factory produced pink honey. Cola-flavored honey was found in hives near tourist attractions. The bees had drunk the nectar found in empty soft drink bottles. Chocolate-flavored honey was found in hives near a candy factory. Bees in orange groves produce orange-flavored honey. Bees in areas of multiple flower sources produce honey of complex flavors.

Honey ranges from colorless, to white, to almost black, with tints of orange, yellow, amber, green, and even blue produced. Lighter-colored honey commands higher prices and tends to have a more delicate flavor than the darker types. Honey quality is judged by color, flavor, and aroma. Fermented honey becomes *mead,* a drink long known to civilization.

An old custom that originated in ancient times is the practice of placing a few drops of honey on the first book presented to a child. The child would lick off the book, thus forever associating books with sweetness. Nobody disputes the role of the dog as man's best friend, but a convincing argument can also be made for the honeybee.

Choice Cod

We couldn't resist putting this food words trivia item in the book: If you turn this book upside down and look into a mirror at it, you will be able to read the words

CHOICE COD

properly, while the rest of the page is upside-down and backwards.

Afterword

*The discovery of a new dish does more
for the happiness of mankind
than the discovery of a star.*

Anthelme Brillat-Savarin

Mark Twain wrote that after millions of years of evolution the oyster finally appeared. The oyster thought that there was no point in further development; the pinnacle—itself—had obviously been reached. As we eat our Oysters Rockefeller it may occur to us that each generation thinks it has arrived at the peak, the acme of development. Nothing more can be done. The French named an ice cream concoction parfait (perfect) because after that nothing better could possibly be created using ice cream. That was in 1677.

When the cold war ended in 1990, someone opined that history ended with it; nothing more could happen after that. When Picasso died some thought that modern art was buried with him. Where else could abstraction or art in general go? An early director of the United States Patent Office once suggested that the office be abolished, because everything that could possibly be invented, had already been invented, and it was obvious, (at least to him) that further inventions would not be forthcoming.

Fortunately for writers about food, nobody in the food business has yet made such doleful predictions. There are good reasons for this. The end of food, or the end of cuisine, would mean the end of civilization, unless we are to eat pills in the future instead of steaks and pasta. Food is as unending, we assume, as the horizon. Americans, in any case, are a nation of futurologists, never content with the past or the present, always peeking ahead to seek out the latest development in every area of life.

The reputation of the United States as a melting pot of immigrants has provided a second, and unexpected melting pot: the kitchen. To the great joy of gourmets and food adventurers, the cuisines of America's immigrants has brought forth an almost endless cornucopia of new foods and styles of cooking to explore. Growth is the engine of food: the growth of plants and animals each year, the growth and development of food and agricultural technology, the growth of new restaurants and chefs, new food styles and ways of preparation. The world of food is reserved for enthusiasts and optimists; pessimists don't eat well.

There will doubtless be an unending supply of new trends and fads for foodies to explore, but the history of food will not be made in kitchens in the early part of the next century. Muckrakers and gadflies are in good supply to prod and push the food industry. We have been warned of pesticide residues on fruits and vegetables, and iconoclasts like Philip Sokolof spend millions of dollars of their own money taking on giants such as Nabisco and McDonald's to make them stop using artery-clogging oils that cause heart attacks. They are making headway. The nation's second largest movie theater chain, AMC, now sells popcorn with Promise, an oil containing ten percent saturated fat, as compared with butter or tropical oil, which are up to ninety-two percent saturated fats. Dunkin' Donuts is now making some of their doughnuts without egg yolks, which will eliminate ninety percent of the saturated fats. Other companies, stung by loss of patronage from increasingly knowledgeable consumers, are making similar changes for the better.

Genetic engineering will produce wonders in the next few years. In 1988 a team of researchers at Cornell University mapped the genome of rice. Since then, experiments have been underway using rice protoplasts (cells from which the walls have been removed to allow the manipulation of genes) to develop new strains of rice that will resist diseases and pests, grow larger grains, and have stronger stalks to support the larger grains. Tomatoes and other vegetables are being developed that will be larger, more colorful, and more nutritious.

Genetic engineering can produce similar wonders in animals, making meat tenderer, tastier, and leaner. Nothing is beyond imagination. Someday soon we may see giant oranges, corn kernels as big as eggs, vegetables and fruits in designer colors. An onion is under development that will keep in a refrigerator for six months and taste as fresh as when it was plucked from the ground. Sweet onions will become the norm. It will be possible to fiddle with the hotness of peppers, change their size and color, and make them more important in our diet than they already are.

Catfish, tilapia, lobsters and shrimps are now farmed scientifically, away from the polluted bays of modern cities, in pure water, and are already being sold in markets around the country. The next century will see fish farming become a major agribusiness, growing all sorts of fish, crustaceans, and mollusks under ideal conditions, and with new sizes, colors, and tastes.

Advances in air-freight and storage techniques make it possible to buy exotic fruits and vegetables from distant lands. Just as the microwave, flash-freezing, the food processor, and other inventions have changed eating habits and widened opportunities for the preparation of food in the past few years, new inventions still on the drawing boards will continue to amaze us and make life easier in the kitchen and restaurant.

The steady televising of famous chefs will continue, building an archive of food lore that will prove invaluable for cooks, home-makers, economists, and historians in the near future. Imagine if today we could watch a video tape of Escoffier, who cooked for King George V, circa 1911, or Antonin Carême, master chef at the Royal Pavilion in Brighton, who created memorable meals for the Prince Regent, circa 1817, showing us how they prepared their famous dishes. What a treasure trove of culinary knowledge is being created week-by-week on television!

While the shape of the future can be dimly seen from what is happening now, the details must remain a mystery. Who will be the famous chefs and restaurateurs of the future? What will be the next development in the maturing cuisine of the United States and other countries? What are the specifics of the vegetables and fruits and meats to come? How will the new developments affect the life of the average American?

If famine and starvation can be eliminated, and if the growth of populations around the world can be contained, the preparation and consumption of food likely will increase in importance as entertainment, art, science, and pastime, as it already has in some parts of the developed world.

Pliny the Elder, in the first century A.D., said that, "The stomach is the teacher of the arts and the dispenser of invention." As the present millennium closes, his prophecy is coming closer to fulfillment.

Bibliography

For the reader interested in learning more about some of the subjects discussed in this book, the following books are suggested as starting points:

Aylesworth, Thomas G. *The Alchemists*. Reading, Pa.: Wesley Pub., 1973.

Babor, Thomas. *Alcohol—Customs and Rituals*. New York: Chelsea House Publishers, 1986.

Brown, Sanborn. *Benjamin Thompson, Count Rumford*. Cambridge, Mass.: M.I.T. Press, 1979.

Callen, Anna Teresa. *Wonderful World of Pizzas, Quiches, and Savory Pies*. New York: Crown Publishers, 1981.

Clifton, Claire. *Edible Flowers*. New York: McGraw Hill, 1984.

Cosman, Madeleine Pelner. *Fabulous Feasts*. New York: G. Braziller, 1976.

Crane, Eva. *A Book of Honey*. New York: Scribner's, 1980.

Cusumano, Camille. *The New Foods*. New York: Henry Holt, 1989.

Dickson, Paul. *The Great American Ice Cream Book*. New York: Atheneum, 1972.

Edlin, Herbert L. *Plants and Man*. Garden City, N.Y.: The Natural History Press, 1969

Field, Carol. *The Italian Baker*. New York: Harper & Row, 1985.

Ford, Barbara. *Future Food*. New York: Morrow, 1978.

Fredericks, Dr. Carlton, Ph.D. *Psycho-Nutrition*. New York: Grosset & Dunlap, 1976.

Freeman, Morton. *The Story Behind the Word*. Philadelphia: ISI Press, 1985.

Funk, Wilfred. *Word Origins and Their Romantic Stories*. New York: Funk & Wagnalls Company, 1950.

Griggs, Barbara (Van Der Zee). *The Food Factor*. London/New York: Viking, 1986.

Grigson, Jane. *The Mushroom Feast*. New York: Knopf, 1975.

Hendrickson, Robert. *Lewd Food*. Radnor, PA.: Chilton, 1974.

Hippisley-Coxe, Antony, and Araminta Hippisley-Coxe. *Book Of Sausages*. London: Victor Gollancz, Ltd., in association with W. P. Crawley, 1987.

Ickis, Marguerite. *The Book of Religious Holidays and Celebrations.* New York: Dodd, Mead, 1966.

Johnson, Hugh. *The World Atlas of Wine.* London: Mitchell Beazley Publishers, Ltd., 1979.

Lang, George. *Lang's Compendium of Culinary Nonsense & Trivia.* New York: C. N. Potter, Pub., Dist. by Crown Pub., 1980.

Lasky, Michael S. *The Complete Junk Food Book.* New York: McGraw Hill, 1977

Larsen, Egon. *Food, Past, Present & Future.* London: Fredric Muller, Ltd., 1977.

Marteka, Vincent. *Mushrooms Wild and Edible.* New York: W. W. Norton & Co., 1980.

Mennell, Stephen. *All Manners of Foods.* Oxford, U. K. and New York: Basil Blackwell, Ltd., 1985.

Nelson, Kay Shaw. *Yogurt Cookery—Good and Gourmet.* Washington, New York: Robert B. Luce, Inc., 1972.

Paisner, Milton. *One Word Leads to Another.* New York: Dembner Books, dist. by W. W. Norton, 1982.

Panati, Charles. *Extraordinary Origins of Everyday Things.* New York: Perennial Library, Harper & Row, 1987.

Pearl, Anita May. *Completely Cheese.* Middle Village, New York: Jonathan David Pub., 1978.

Proulx, E. Annie, and Lew Nichols. *The Complete Dairy Foods Cookbook.* Emmaus, PA.: Rodale Press, 1982.

Rinzler, Carol Ann. *The Complete Book of Food.* New York: World Almanac, Pharos Books, 1987.

Root, Waverley Lewis. *Food.* New York: Simon and Shuster, 1980.

Slomon, Evelyne. *The Pizza Book.* New York: New York Times Books, 1984.

Tannahill, Reay. *Food in History.* New York: Crown Pub., 1989.

Tuleja, Tad. *Curious Customs.* New York: Harmony Books, Crown Pub., 1987.

Visser, Margaret. *Much Depends on Dinner.* New York: Grove Press, 1987.

Wasson, R. Gordon. Soma, *Divine Mushroom of Immortality.* New York: Harcourt Brace Jovanovich, 1968

Index

Index

Ice boxes, 22
Ice cream, history of, 101–105
Ice houses, 14
Insects, 161–162
Italy
    breads of, 148–151
    cooking style of, 18
    gelato developed in, 101–102
    wines of, 15–16

Jackson, Caleb, 82–83
Jell-O, 29
Jerusalem artichokes, 57–58
Junk food, 124–126

Kellogg, John and Will, 83–84
Ketchup, 58
Kitchen, 58
Kiwi, about, 58
Kuchenmeisterey, 17

La Cuisinière Bourgeoise (Menon), 21
La Physiologie de Goût (Brillat-
    Savarin), 23
Lahner, Georg, 21–22
Le Cuisinièr Francois (Varenne), 19
Lead, in foods, 115, 154
Leeks, 17, 58, 108
Les Dons De Comus (Marin), 21
Lobster Newburg, 59
Louis XIV, king of France, 113–114
Lucullus, 16

McCann, Al, 127–128
Maple sugar and syrup, 173–175
Margarine, 27, 59
Marketing of foods, first, 14
Marmalade, 59–60
Mars, Franklin, 31
Meat
    cultural differences regarding,
        141–143
    designer, 142–143
    -packing plants, 26
    shipping of, 27

Medicinal uses of foods, 4, 13–14,
    122–123, 129
Melba toast, 60
Metchnikoff, Elie, 87
Mice, as food, 162–163
Microwave ovens, 31
Middle Ages
    alcohol in, 41–42
    feasts of, 138–141, 152
Milk, evaporated, 24
Modern Cook The (Francatelli), 24
Montagu, John, 64
Moore, Thomas, 22
Mrs. Beecher's Domestic Receipt Book,
    24
Muesli, 85–86
Mushrooms, about, 190–195
Mutton, 60

Napoleon I, 2, 22–23
National foods, 6–7
Nutrition
    Denmark experience with,
        154–155
    Thompson on, 165–166
Nuts
    assumptions about, 3–4
    cashew, 54
    filbert, 56
    Macadamia, 59
    pecan, 62
    walnut, 67

Oculinum, 129
Onions, 12
    etymology of word, 60
    properties of, 14, 16, 33, 109,
        115–116
Oranges, 60–61
Organic farming, 33
Oysters, 61

Paprika, 61
Pasteur, Louis, 25–26
Pasteurization, 26

Index